# Secret Places In The Mojave Desert Volume IV

(Joshua Tree & The Mojave)

by Jim Mattern (aka: Death Valley Jim)
Photographs by the Author (except where noted)
Cover photo: Hexahedron Mine (Joshua Tree NP)
Back photo: Aiken Arch Pictographs (Mojave NP)

Maps: ©OpenStreetMap contributors

Copyright © 2013 Death Valley Jim

All rights reserved. No part of this publication may be reproduced, stored in a retrieval system, or transmitted, by any means, electronic, mechanical, photocopying, recording or otherwise – except as permitted under Section 107 or 108 of the United States Copyright Act – without the prior written permission of Death Valley Jim.

SPECIAL THANKS TO THE FOLLOWING:

Meghan Mattern (my loving wife), Sandy & Mike Scafedi, Mike & Deb Moyer, Danielle Moyer, Jonathan Moyer, Jim & Janice Moyer (Grandma & Grandpa), Jim & Tammy Moyer, Crystal Bone, Courtney Russell, Gail Cornelius, Bill Russell (Rest in Peace), Vinch, Stephen Brown, John Acosta III, Jacob Gieger, Chris Morano, Mike Behrman (joshuatreecamping.com), Marsha Lewis, Lore Vineyard, Neenah SpellPerson, Jan Iwashita, Stuart Burgess, Paul Charron (Building in the Past), Russell Hartill, Carlos Esparza (Esparza Family Restaurant), Ken Hooper, Janet Morgan, Amina Anderson (Beatty Museum), John Grasson (Dezert Magazine), Kern County Historical Society, Bigs Sunflower Seeds, Honey Stinger, Carnivore Candy, Somersault Snacks, The Stagecoach Hotel & Casino (Beatty, NV), ORV Watch Kern County, Eastern Kern Historical Society, Jeffrey Spivey, Barbara Zaragoza, Rajan Parrikar, Aleksandr Stzhalkovski, Ryan Halub, Ken Johnson, Martin Jespersen, Gary Speck, and all of my desert family that have purchased my books, and follow my website and Facebook page!

Thanks to the following Facebook fans: Russell Hartill, Bobbie Lassiter, Victoria Amerson, Tresa Denney, PhotoJeeper, Kristian Paul Castellano, Sherry L. Roberts, Linda Becker, John Bevan Jr., Patrick Duchow, JoAnn Newbury, Ross S. Heckmann. Gail Marie Loveland, Jack Cook, Penny Hogan, Barbara Lyn Hinkey, Cris Mateski, Jack Anthony Rook, Jason Becker, Linda Becker, Bill Matula, Terry Fisk, Dianna Sherrick, Donna Utegg, Greg Myers, Andrew St Laurent, Brenda Morris, Dean Cofield, Larry Riendeau, Bob Goodwin, Carmen Prater, Dennis Carroll, Craig Williams, Elliot Koeppel

# Table of Contents:

| | |
|---|---|
| Desert Travel Essentials | 1 |
| Mojave Desert Animal Track Guide | 2 |
| Etiquette for Visiting a Petroglyph / Pictograph Site | 5 |

**JOSHUA TREE** — 7
- 49 Palm Canyon Oasis — 8
- Alister's Cave Pictographs — 10
- "Bloody Hands" Pictographs — 12
- Coyote Hole Rock Art Site — 14
- Diamond Solstice Pictographs — 16
- "Disney" Pictographs — 18
- Eagle Cliff Mine — 20
- Gold Park Mining District — 23
- Hensen Well — 27
- Hexahedron Mine — 29
- "High Noon" Pictographs — 32
- Ivanhoe Mine — 35
- O.K. Mine — 37
- Pleasant Valley Petroglyphs — 40
- Queen Valley Pictograph Boulder — 42
- Red & Brunette Ladies Pictographs — 44
- Samuelson's Rocks — 46
- Slab Rock Shelter Pictographs — 48
- Virginia Dale Mine — 50
- Wall Street Mill — 53
- Wonderland Ranch (Ohlson House) — 56

**JOHNSON & LUCERNE VALLEY**
- Black Lava Butte Petroglyphs — 60
- Hondo Wash Rock Art Site — 63
- King Clone Creosote Ring — 66
- Lester Dale Mine — 68
- Rodman Mountain Grand Canyon — 71
- Spanish Smelter — 74
- Viscera Spring / Vaughn Spring — 76
- Yaranka Canyon Petroglyphs — 78

THE MOJAVE NATIONAL PRESERVE 81
    Bert Smith Rock Cabin 82
    Big Horn Mine 84
    Black Tank Wash / Aiken Arch Rock Art Site 87
    Camp Rock Springs Petroglyphs 90
    Counsel Rock Archaeological Site 92
    Fort Piute / Beale 95
    Indian Well Petroglyphs 98
    Maruba / Ledge 101
    Mary's Cave Pictographs 103
    Piute Creek Petroglyphs 105
    Providence / Bonanza King Mine 109
    Woods Wash Rock Art Site 113

# Desert Travel Essentials

The following are all items that you should carry with you when you are traveling in the desert. The list may sound like a lot, but in a worst case scenario you would want to prepared. If you are not prepared you are risking your life, as well anyones life that may be traveling with you. This is in no way a complete list, but a good starting point.

Water - You can never bring to much! Some people recommend a gallon of water per person per day. I personally recommend a 5 gallon jug for every two people in your party per day.

Food - Always carry extra food that can last you a day or two. I keep enough prepackaged beef jerky with me to last a few days. It is light weight and compact. Self-Heating MRE's are also a wonderful option to keep packed in your vehicle for an emergency meal.

Shovel - My shovel stays in my vehicle at all times, even when I'm just cruising around town. You never know when you might get stuck.

Gasoline - There are long stretches of backcountry roads, and many times a gas station can be over a hundred miles away. Having some extra gasoline with you as a precaution is a good thing.

Outdoor GPS or Compass- Handheld Outdoor GPS is the only GPS that you should trust in the desert. Make sure it is loaded with topographical maps of the area that you are traveling, and make sure you know how to read a topographical map. DO NOT RELY ON YOUR VEHICLES GPS DEVICE.

Spare Tire or Two - No explanation needed. Don't forget the jack!

Matches/Lighter - Something that will allow you to start a fire easily.

Signal flares or mirror - Anything that might get the attention of an airplane flying overhead, or another motorist that you may see at a distance.

Knife or Multitool - A knife can come in handy in many situations. From skinning an animal (if needed), to using it to help build a shelter, or even using it as a signaling device.

First Aid Kid - Injuries happen when we least expect it. Be prepared for them! It is also important in a desert situation that you add a snake bite kit to your first aid kit.

Blanket/Warm Clothing - In the spring, winter and fall months temperatures at night can get downright cold. Sometimes well below freezing! Don't let the warm daytime temperatures fool you, and always be prepared for colder weather.

# Mojave Desert Animal Track Guide

This guide provides you with some of the more common tracks that you may encounter while exploring in the Mojave Desert. This is by no means a complete list. Tracks are not to scale.

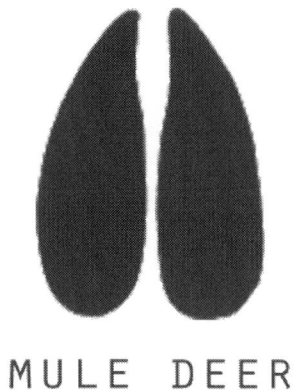

MULE DEER

COTTENTAIL RABBIT

MOUNTAIN LION

DEER MOUSE

BADGER

GREY FOX

BOBCAT

RINGTAIL
(MINER'S CAT)

COYOTE

RAVEN

BIGHORN
SHEEP

ROADRUNNER

# Etiquette for Visiting a Petroglyph / Pictograph Site

Petroglyphs & Pictographs are fragile, non-renewable cultural resources that, once damaged, can never be replaced.

By remembering and following the rules listed here, you can help preserve these unique and fragile cultural resources that are part of our heritage.

Avoid Touching the Petroglyphs & Pictographs

Look and observe, BUT DO NOT TOUCH! Preserve petroglyphs & pictographs by not touching them in any way. Even a small amount of the oils from our hands can erode petroglyphs & pictographs and destroy the patina (color) of the carved, pecked or painted image.

When climbing among the rocks be careful, you can dislodge loose stones causing damage to the petroglyph & pictograph boulders. Falling rocks may scratch the carved and pecked images causing unintentional damage. Do not re-arrange the rocks or move things from where you find them. The petroglyphs & pictographs are important individually and in relation to each other. To even try and understand a petroglyph or pictograph it needs to be viewed in relation to its environment: including the adjacent image(s), the entire basalt escarpment, and the surrounding landscape. For someone to fully appreciate a site, the glyphs and their surroundings should be left undisturbed.

Do not introduce any foreign substance to enhance the carved, pecked or painted images for photographic or drawing purposes. Altering, defacing, or damaging the petroglyphs is against the law — even if the damage is unintentional.

Re-pecking or re-painting does not restore a petroglyph or pictograph, it destroys the original. DO NOT add your own marks to the images. The introduction of graffiti destroys the petroglyphs & pictographs and is disrespectful to contemporary Native Americans and their ancestors.

Don't remove the petroglyphs & pictographs! It is against the law to remove items from prehistoric or geologic sites. Such vandalism carries a fine and penalty.

# Joshua Tree National Park
(Including locations outside of the park boundaries)

# 49 Palm Canyon Oasis

GPS Coordinates:  34° 6'22.65"N 116° 6'19.95"W

Trail Head: 34° 7'9.48"N 116° 6'43.37"W

To access the 49 Palms Canyon Oasis a hike of 1.5 miles is required (3 mile round trip). The parking area is located at the end of Canyon Road. From Highway 62 outside of the town of Twentynine Palms there are signs marking the turn for the canyon.

This three-mile out and back hike has been classified by the National Park Service as moderately strenuous, and rightfully so. The trail leads you up 300 feet along a ridge in a short distance. As you wind along the ridge you have stunning views of the city of Twentynine Palms and the canyons below. Nearing the one mile mark you will begin seeing the Palm Oasis in the distance. From here you have a steep 300 foot climb down into the canyon.

The trail is well-defined, the Park Service have built steps out of local stones in the steepest sections. Be sure to bring plenty of water on this trekk, the temperature soars and there is no shaded areas available until you reach the oasis.

The oasis was used by Native American tribes long before the settlement of white men in the area. Much like the people of today they were drawn to the area for its lush green palm trees, water, and shade. They would also harvest the dates from the palms, they used the dates as a source of sugar. The oasis also served as a hunting grounds to the Natives, big horn sheep and other animals utilized the oasis as a watering source. If you are lucky you may still come across a heard of big horns today.

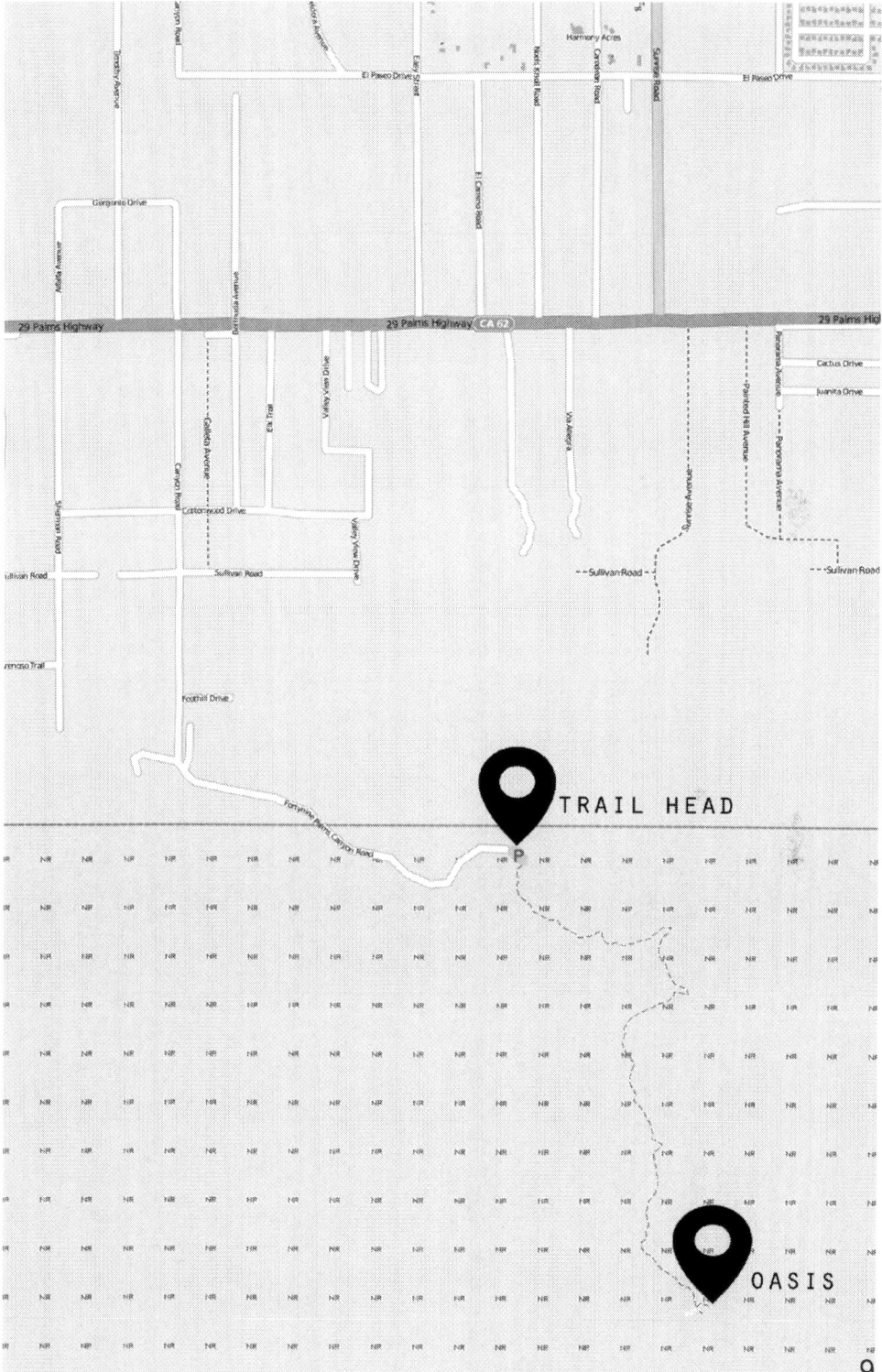

# Alister's Cave Pictographs

## GPS Coordinates:   34° 1'54.79"N 116° 8'59.81"W

The Alister's Cave Pictograph and Petroglyph site is located in the Wonderland of Rocks, just a short distance from the popular Barker Dam attraction, as well as popular boulder climbing spots. The cave is signed by the Park Service to prevent climbing at this particular location, but you won't find the location on maps, and park employees won't speak of it.

Despite its name, it isn't really a cave, but rather a rock shelter. The shelter is covered from top to bottom with many hundred faded pictograph designs. Some designs can be made out without enhancement, but it is difficult to see what you are looking at. The paint colors used are red, white, black, and grey.

There are both pictographs and petroglyphs present, but the pictographs far outweigh the petroglyphs. The petroglyphs are isolated to only one small section of the shelter floor.

Having spent roughly an hour at the shelter on a warm 95° day, it quickly became apparent why the Natives enjoyed this location. Lounging on the shelter floor, protected by the shade the temperature was much more enjoyable than being directly in the sun. It felt as if there was at least a 15° – 20° temperature difference.

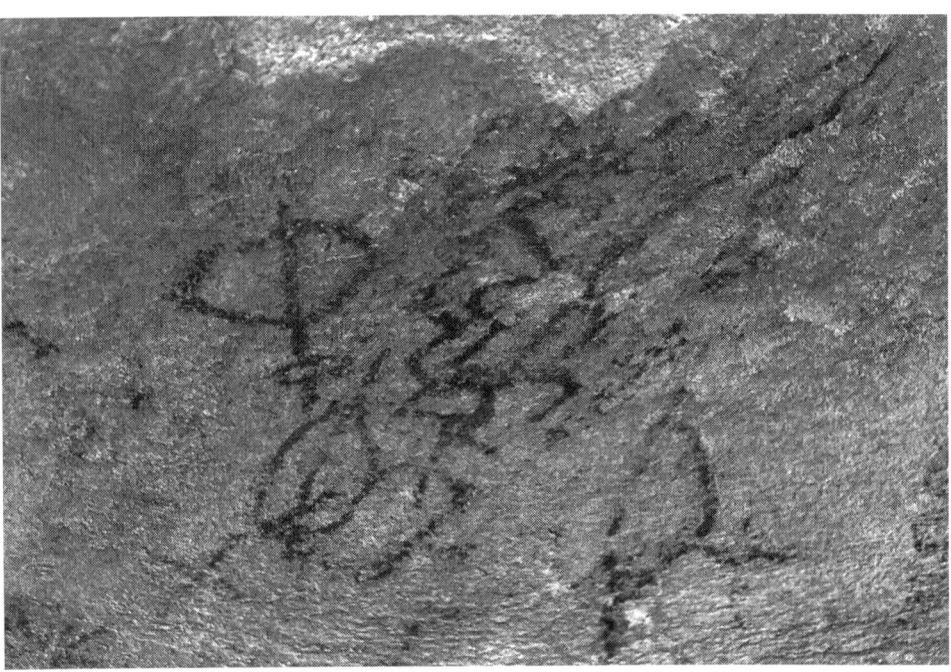

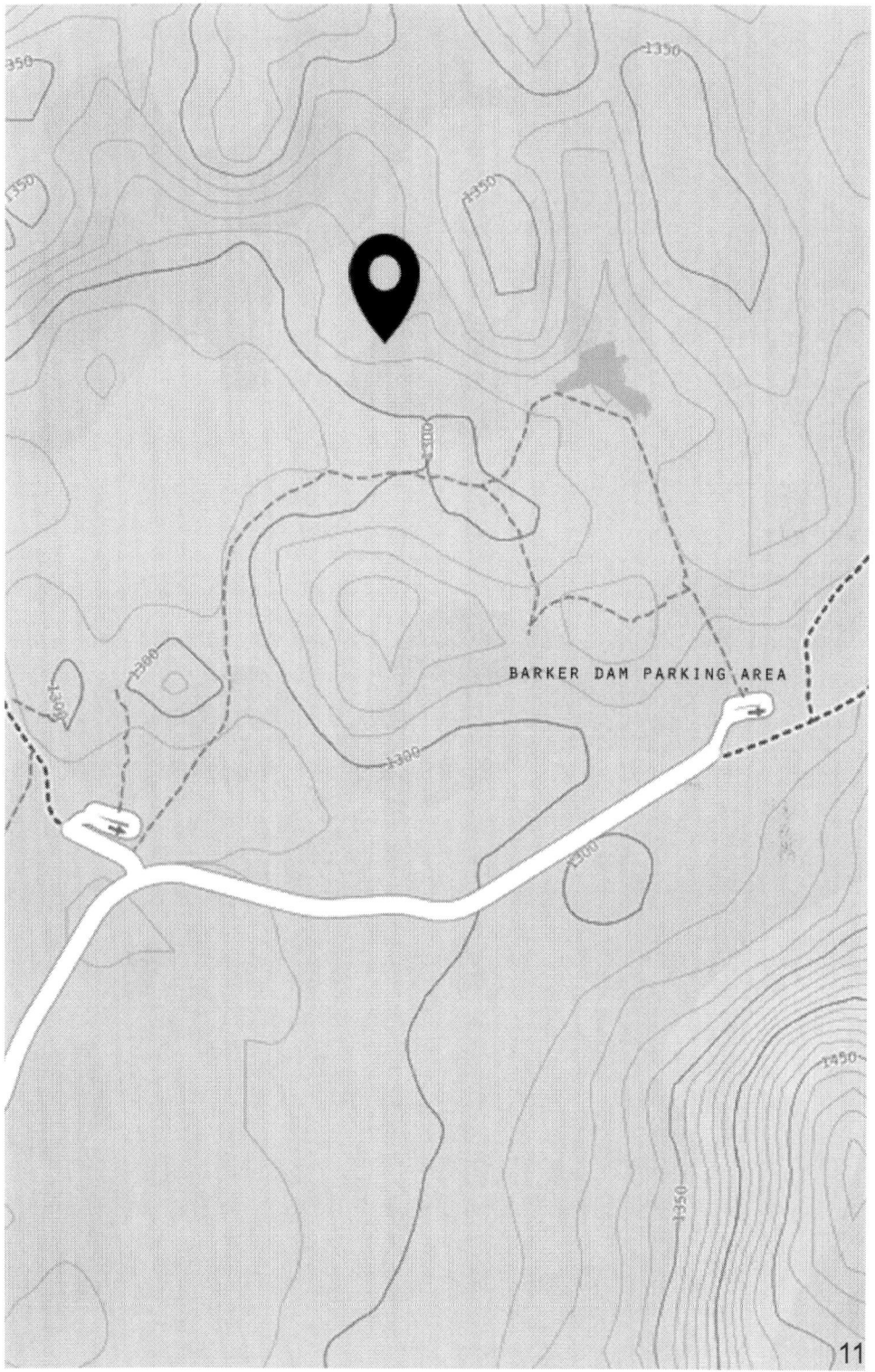

# "Bloody Hands" Pictographs
## GPS Coordinates:   34° 1'54.30"N 116° 8'57.96"W

I stumbled upon this small pictograph site while on the search for the Alister's Cave Pictographs in the Wonderland of Rocks.

These pictographs and one petroglyph are located on the lower part of a boulder that has a small overhang, which has protected the pictographs somewhat from the elements. The pictograph designs are painted in red.

Due to the close proximity of the Alister's Cave site, these designs had likely been created by the same person or persons.

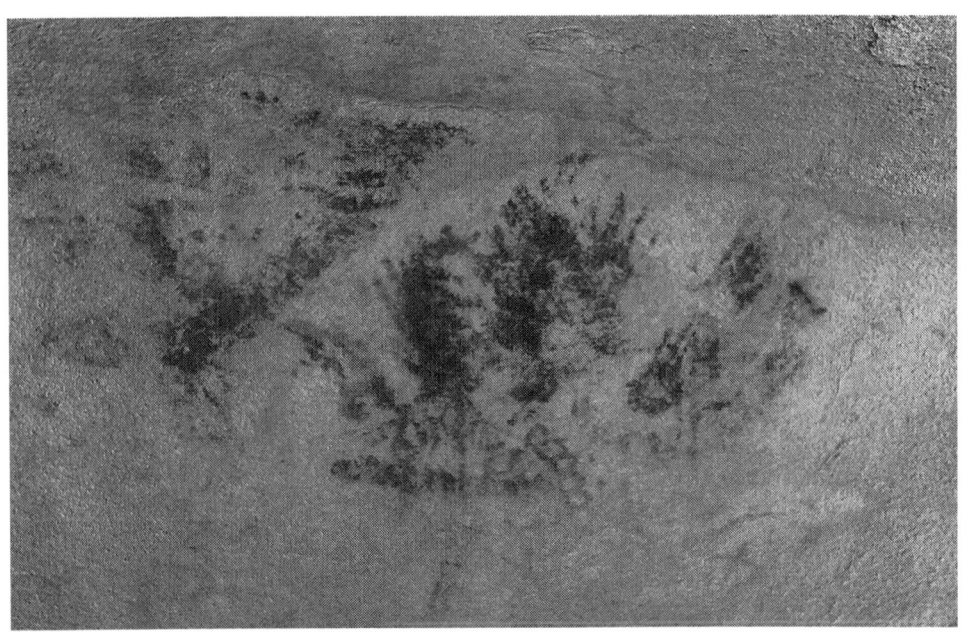

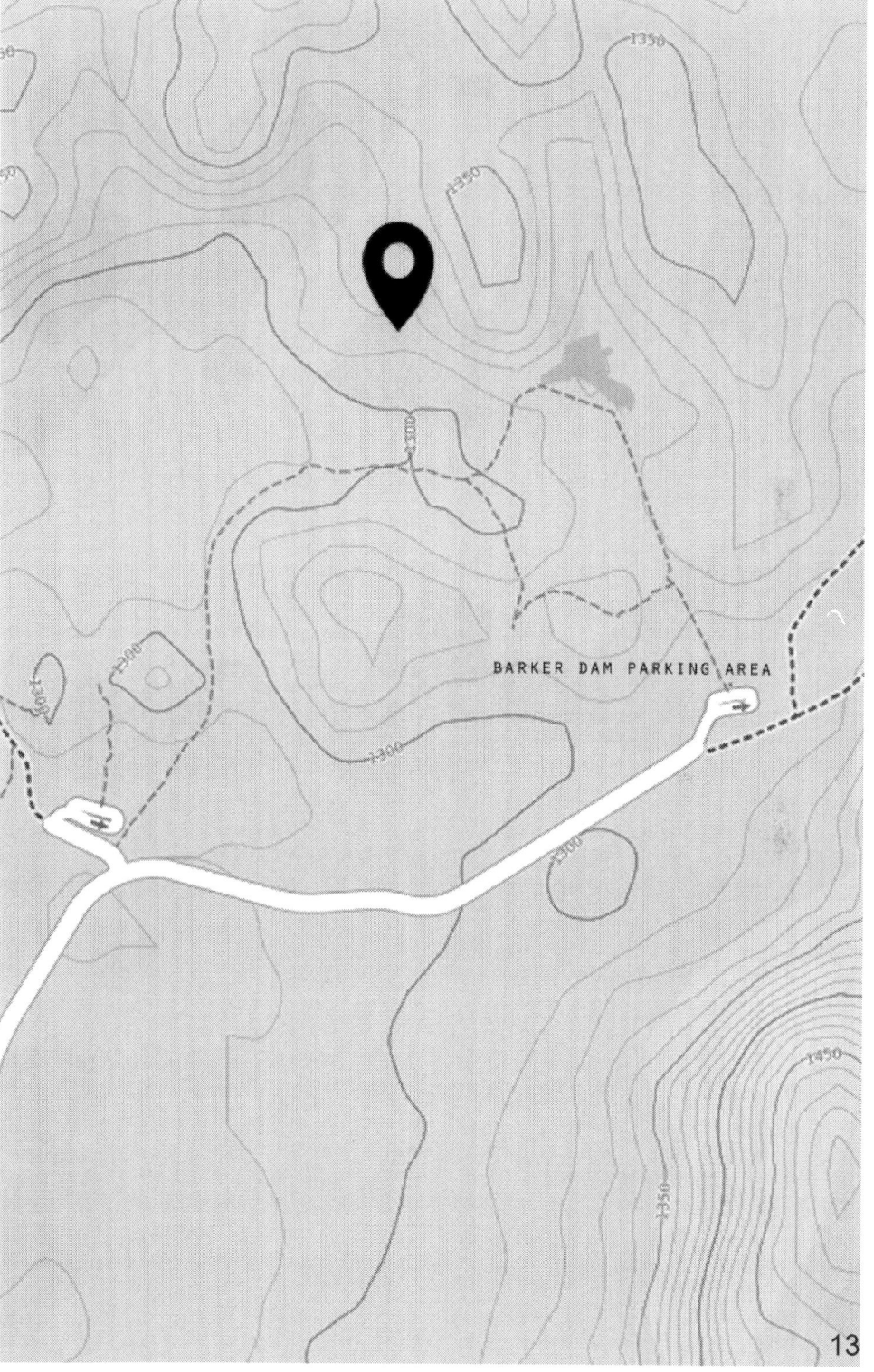

# Coyote Hole Rock Art Site

## GPS Coordinates:    34° 7'5.15"N 116°18'31.32"W

Nestled in a sandy wash just a few short miles from downtown Joshua Tree is a treasure that is hidden from the thousands of tourist that traverse the area on any given week. An estimated 50-75 Serrano petroglyphs line the tall stone walls of the canyon, as well at least one nice sized barely visible pictograph.

A majority of the well-preserved petroglyphs are located high above the wash floor on the tall walls surrounding the wash. The petroglyphs that are at a lower level are much more difficult to make out due to both natural deterioration as well as man-made destruction.

The designs located at Coyote Hole are of the Great Basin Abstract Style. They consist of anthropomorphs (Attribution of human motivation, characteristics, or behavior to inanimate objects, animals, or natural phenomena) and quadrupeds (A four-footed animal). The area was known to be occupied by the Serrano, as well possibly the Chemehuevi and the Cahuilla.

A single pictograph panel lies within the wash, I happened to find it by chance while visually scouring the canyon walls.

In the 1960's the Army Corps of Engineers blasted away a majority of the lower level petroglyphs in order to use the stone for the construction of a drainage canal underneath a local highway.

Recent vandalization has also become a problem. Coyote Hole has become an area for local parties which has posed a threat to both the natural beauty of the wash as well as the ancient art. Spray paint now covers some of the stone walls, as well as bullet holes. Local organizations have begun to do regular patrols and clean ups.

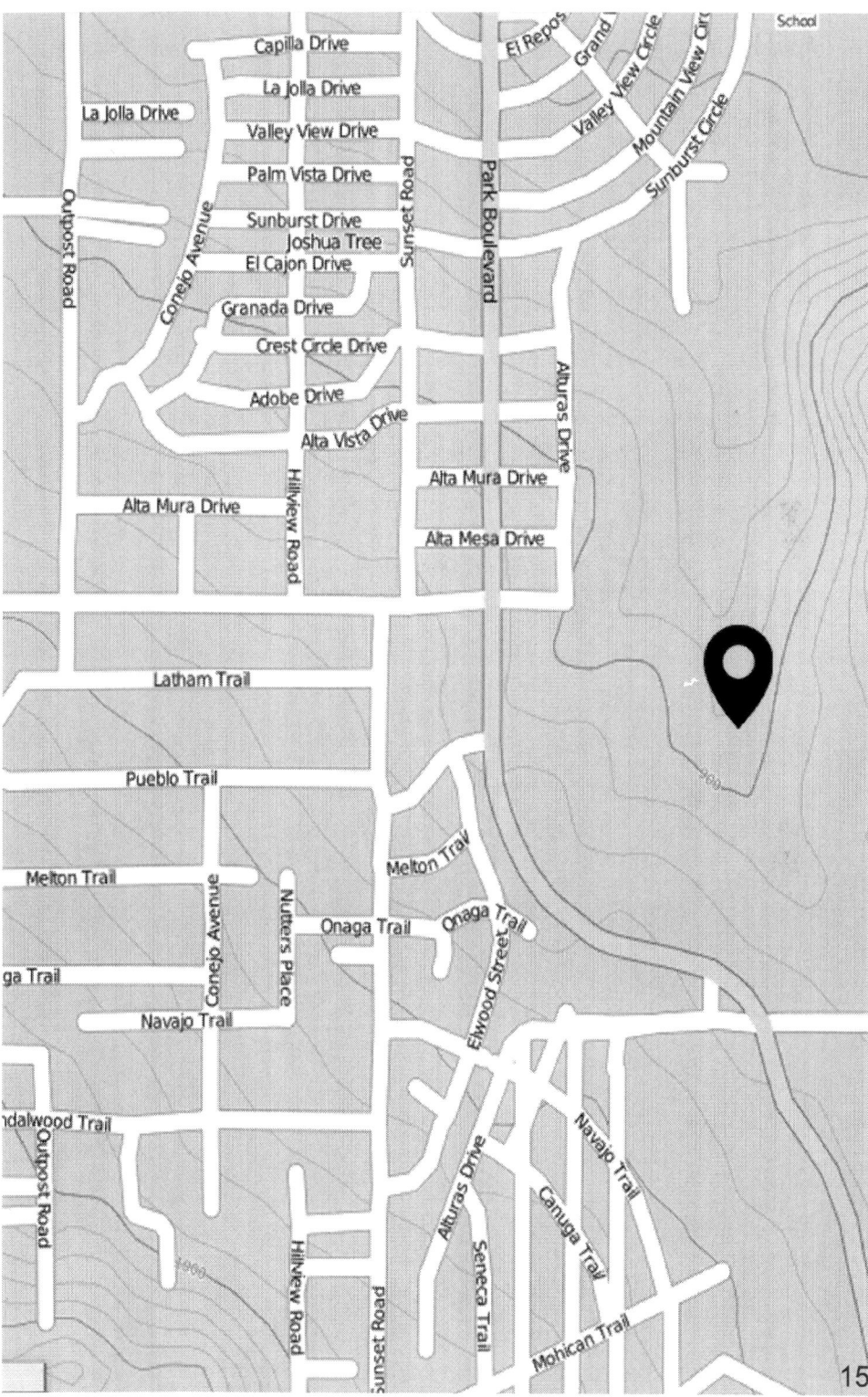

# Diamond Solstice Pictographs

## GPS Coordinates:  34° 1'56.02"N 116° 9'8.41"W

The Diamond Solstice pictograph site is believed by archeologists to be a summer solstice marker.

The Diamond patterns tend to be a representation of a birth canal (IE: vagina), which can translate to the creation of new life. Also present is sunburst design.

Another source provides the following information from a 1984 summer solstice observation at this site, an "intense, vertical, finger-like beam of sunlight" pierced the shadows of the shelter and pointed directly to the sunburst motif. Consequently, it's thought that this site may have been used by shamans to predict this important seasonal cycle which is tied to the food supply of the culture. It would have been the shaman's duty to watch, interpret and if necessary to intervene with the appropriate supernatural magic to maintain the seasonal balance which was so important.

Hidden in a low recess of the rock wall, there is a panel of tally marks, twenty-nine in all. They are faded badly, but still visible.

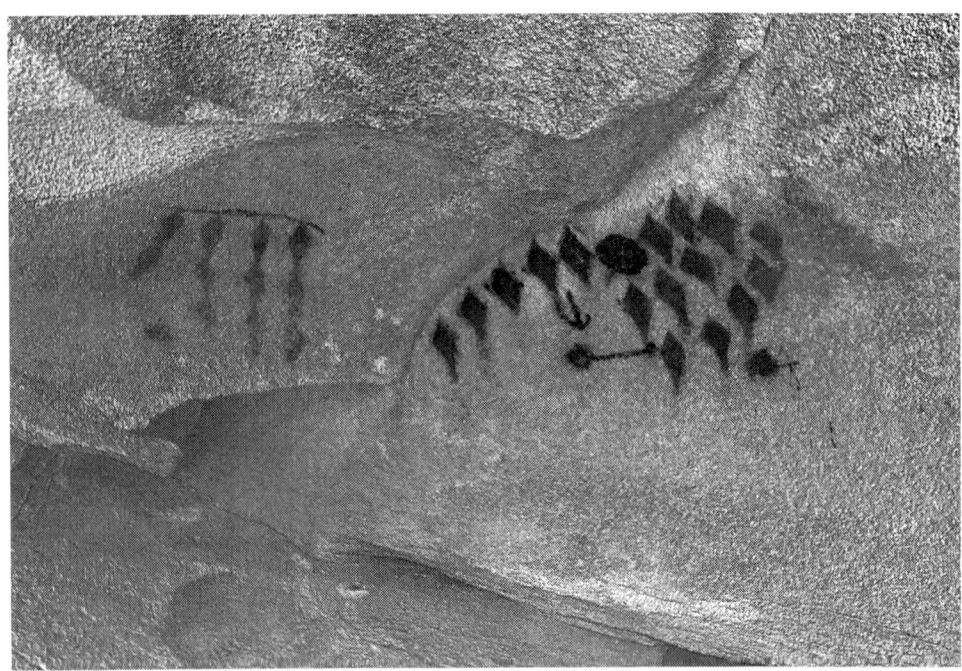

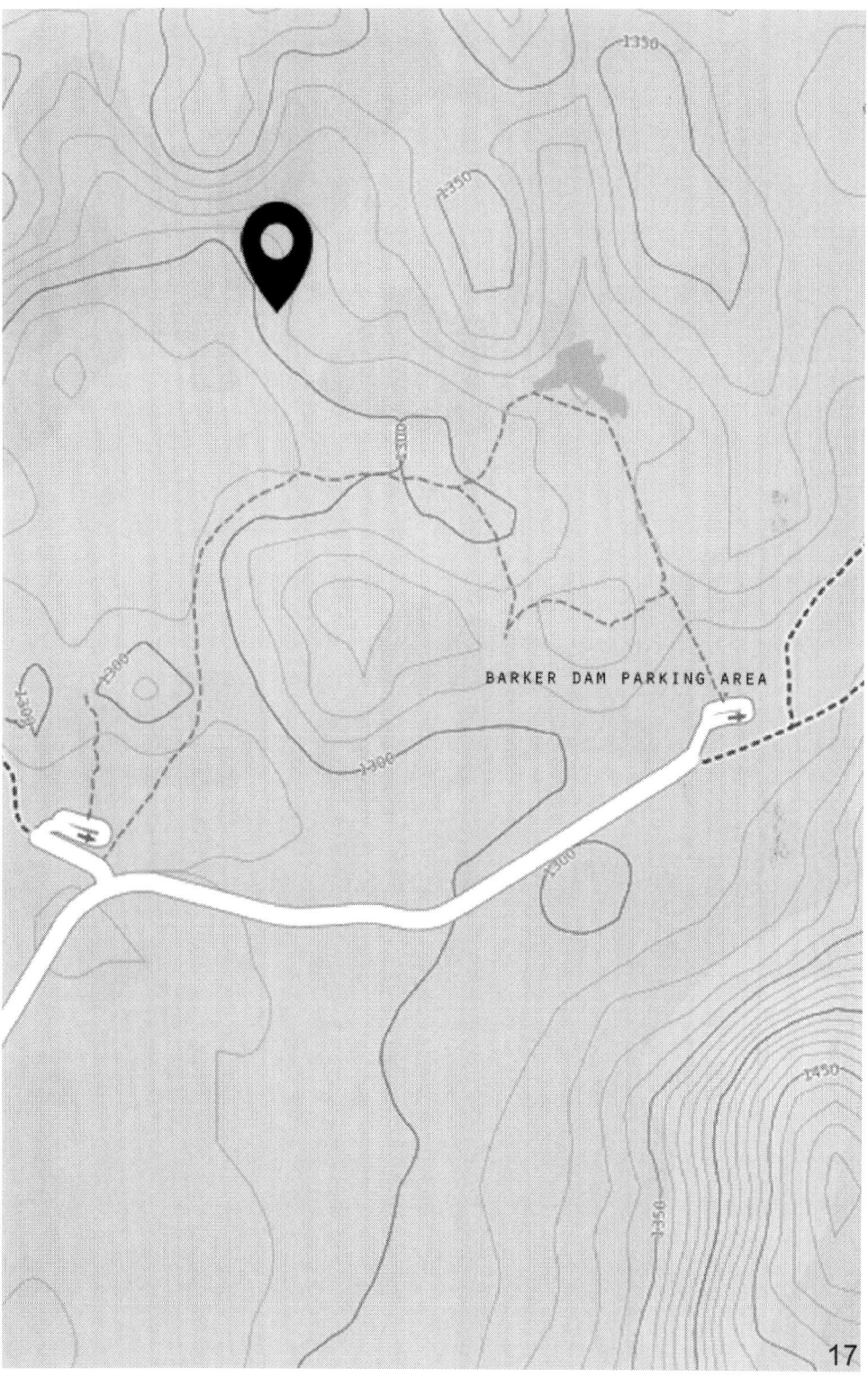

# "Disney" Pictographs

GPS Coordinates:  34° 1'34.24"N 116° 8'49.12"W

The "Disney" Pictographs is the most well-known rock art location within the park. Located just a short distance from the popular tourist attraction, Barker Dam and along the Barker Dam Nature Trail; this site sees plenty of traffic on a daily basis.

The location is made up of authentic petroglyphs, as well as pictographs. However a majority of the pictographs that are visible to the naked eye are a product of the Disney Company. In the late 1950's the popular movie studio shot scenes from the film "Chico, the Misunderstood Coyote" at this site. The designs that originally covered the wall didn't show up well on film, so they opted to paint over the designs to make them more vibrant on film. Some of the "touch up" work also included painting inside of original Native petroglyphs. Today this would be looked at as vandalization, and would not be tolerated.

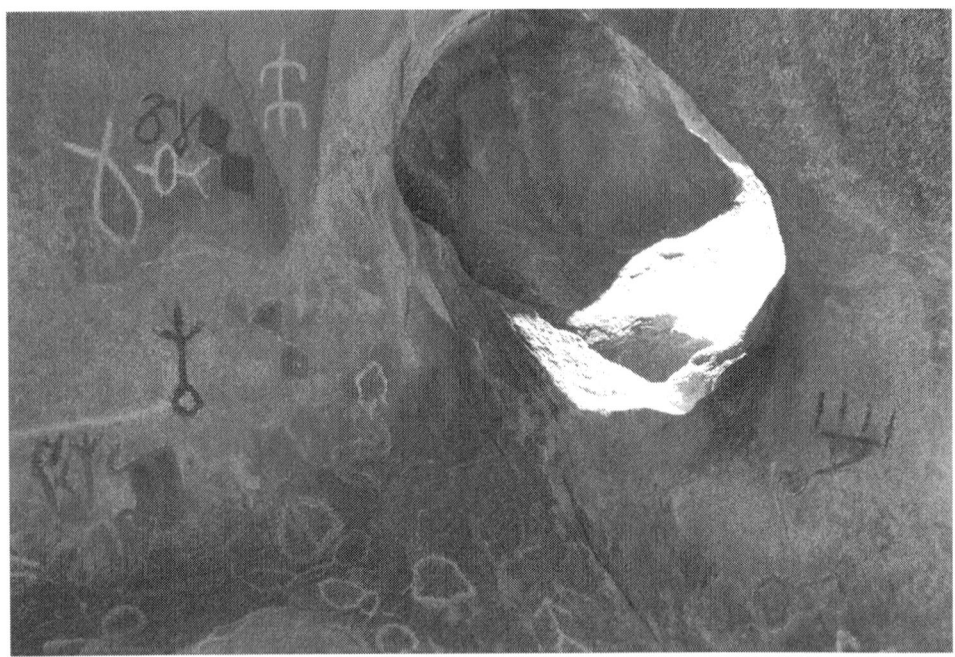

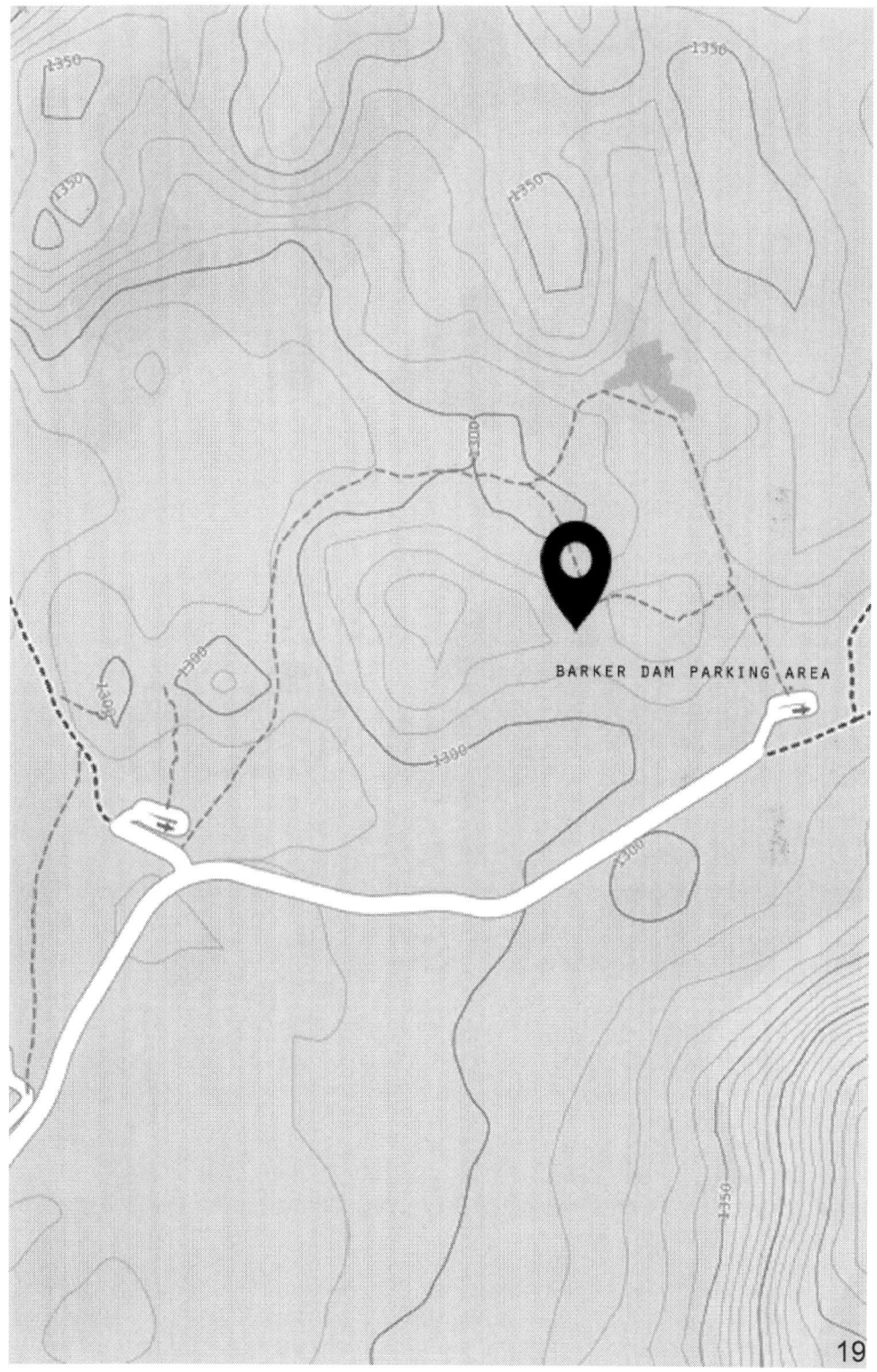

# Eagle Cliff Mine

## GPS Coordinates:  34° 1'20.48"N  116° 3'43.16"W

From the trail head at the Pine City Back Country Board you wind down into a wash, then climb to the top of the ruins of the Desert Queen Mine. Little remains of the Desert Queen with the exception of a couple of pieces of equipment, and caged off mine shafts. The ruins are less than stellar.

From the Desert Queen Mine you continue to wind your way up the mountain side along a landscape that is full of yuccas, cactus, and other desert plants. Large boulders and rock formations are abundant as well. The trail is easy to follow, as past visitors have created cairns (man-made stack of stones) to help guide you along the way. Despite being only a three-mile round trip, it is likely that you won't stumble upon others hiking this route, as its overall remoteness is outside of most people's comfort zone.

Like the Desert Queen, the mine shaft at Eagle Cliff has been caged off by the Park Service. The show stealer here, is the miner's cabin that was built into a rock shelter near the site of the mine shaft. The cabin is stunning, and has been left intact complete with pots, pans, shelving, crates, utensils and more. A stone fireplace that was built to help battle the winter nights still stands in its place.

Little is known about the Eagle Cliff Mine, it does however date back as far as 1895; making it part of the McHaney Mining District, one of the earlier mining districts in the area.

If you decide to visit the Eagle Cliff Mine, please the leave the cabin as you found it. Do not take any of the relics, and be respectful of this wonderful hidden gem.

# Gold Park Mining District

## GPS Coordinates: 34° 1'40.28"N 115°59'11.98"W

The Gold Park Mining District, was part of the earliest inceptions of Joshua Tree National Park, but was removed and placed back into the hands of the BLM after an uproar from locals that still mined recreationally in the historic district.

Mining began in the Gold Park District in the late 1890's, but it wasn't until J.E. Schweng, and his associates formed the Gold Park Consolidated Mining Company in 1905, that any major developments took place.

By 1921 Gold Park Consolidated held 52 claims in the district, while only a handful had been developed.

A 1921 Report by the State Mineralogist for the California State Mining Bureau reported the following:

**Gold Park Group No. 2**

Elevation 2300 feet. This group consists of ten claims. The ore occurs in lenses of quartz at intervals along fractures in a coarse grained granite. The general trend of these veins is N. 10° W. Near the surface the dip is steeply to the east, with depth changing slightly westward. The veins are usually narrow, about 8" to 18" of quartz, but occasionally widening to 6 feet. The gold is free milling and very finely disseminated. Seldom visible to the naked eye. Copper stains occasion ally occur in the quartz, but these disappear usually below 20 foot depth. The workings on this group are mostly superficial, consisting of shallow shafts and trenches. The pay shoots are short, consisting of a maximum length of 60 feet. Said to average $8 to $10 per ton in gold. Developments consist of tunnel 100 feet long, and a number of shafts from 30 to 50 feet deep. Mill, 2 Nissen stamps and Bryan roller mill at Twenty-nine Palms. At mine there is one stamp test mill driven by 5-h.p. gas engine.

**Boss Mine**

A shaft has been sunk to a vertical depth of 122 feet on the vein, and a few feet north of intersection of the main vein striking due N. and S. and a branch striking about S. 10° W. These veins are in the granite. On the 65-foot level the vein was drifted on to the south connecting with a 100-foot shaft. The vein on this level shows a width of 1£ to 2 feet, and was stoped to the surface. At the bottom of shaft a drift was run due north 200 feet, but no pay shoot encountered. There are at least 1000 feet of crosscuts and drifts on this level. The vein formation is about 4' wide, showing 8" of quartz, the remainder consisting of shattered granite and stringers of quartz. Equipment, 7-h.p. gas engine hoist.

## Atlanta Mine

On this claim a narrow vein of quartz occurs in the granite, striking N. 10° E. and dipping almost vertical. The workings consist of shaft and three tunnels of different elevations. The shaft is located near foot of hill and to the south of the tunnels, and was sunk to depth of 100 ft. on a narrow vein. About 100 ft. above the collar of this shaft is the lower tunnel. This was driven N. 10° E. for about 250 ft., about 150 feet from portal raise to upper tunnel and surface. Beyond this raise the tunnel is caved, so was not accessible. Practically no ore is exposed in lower tunnel. Fifty feet above tunnel is the Intermediate tunnel, driven on seam in granite, which opens into a narrow lens of quartz. The shoots of ore developed in these workings were short, but repotted to carry high values in gold.

## Jadonia Mine

Workings on this claim consist of two shafts, sunk on vein to depth of 50 and 100 feet. Vein varies from 24. to 4 feet. The ore extracted from these workings was treated in one stamp mill and reported to have yielded $12 per ton on the plates. The quartz lies between rhyolite and granite foot wall.

## Black Warrior Mine

This is the most southernly mine of the group, lying about 3£ miles south of camp. The mineralization occurs along a shear zone in altered granite. The hanging is a gneiss with a well denned talc wall. General trend of the ore body is N. 10° W. with a dip to the west. Workings consist of a 200-foot shaft sunk on the vein in the center of claim. The quartz in the vein matter is highly oxidized and contains considerable iron and lime. Its black appearance, due to iron and manganese stains, gives it its name. The vein is different from the others of the district, containing considerable pyrite and some arsenopyrite. The dump is said to contain 2200 tons of ore which will assay $14 per ton. The shaft is vertical to 70-foot level, from this point sunk on an incline of 65 degrees east. On 70-foot level a drift run 100 feet N. 45° W., exposing an ore body 60 feet in width. Mineralized zone made up of quartz and brecciated wall rock. On 150' level a crosscut was run for 60 feet west, and is said to be entirely in ore. Equipment, 12-h.p. gas engine hoist ; 8" x 8" compressor. Two men employed on development work.

## Oro Oopio Mine

On this claim the mineralization follows a shear zone, and the granite has been altered to a gneiss. A shaft sunk on vein to depth of 50 feet. Vein strikes N. 10° E. About 150 feet south of this shaft another shaft has been sunk on narrow quartz vein to depth of 100 feet. Vein 2 feet wide, stated average $8 per ton.

Gold Park Consolidated, was the largest holding on the district, they where not the only party to have an interest in the district. Charles Wilson (aka Johnny "Quartz" Wilson, aka "Chuckwalla" Wilson) and Bill McHaney both prospected in the district.

McHaney, lived in the Gold Park District for a better part of 30 years, while he searched for the "lost lode". Even Bill Keys, the most well known and respected miner in the Joshua Tree area owned a mine in the district, the Goat Mine.

During Gold Park's heyday, the district was the home of the Gold Park Hotel, the hotel was moved to its current day location at the 29 Palms Inn in Twentynine Palms in the late 1920s.

Today little remains of the Gold Park Mining District. The structures from the mines and communities are long gone. However, evidence of it's mining past is still evident in the form of tailings, old rusted and shot up vehicles, foundations, and historic garbage dumps filled with rusty cans and broken bottles.

Many of the mines are still open for exploration, and recreational mining continues to take place. For how long, it is unknown. There has been much consideration to reinstate the district into the National Park, if this does happen the mines will quickly be sealed and recreational mining will be become illegal.

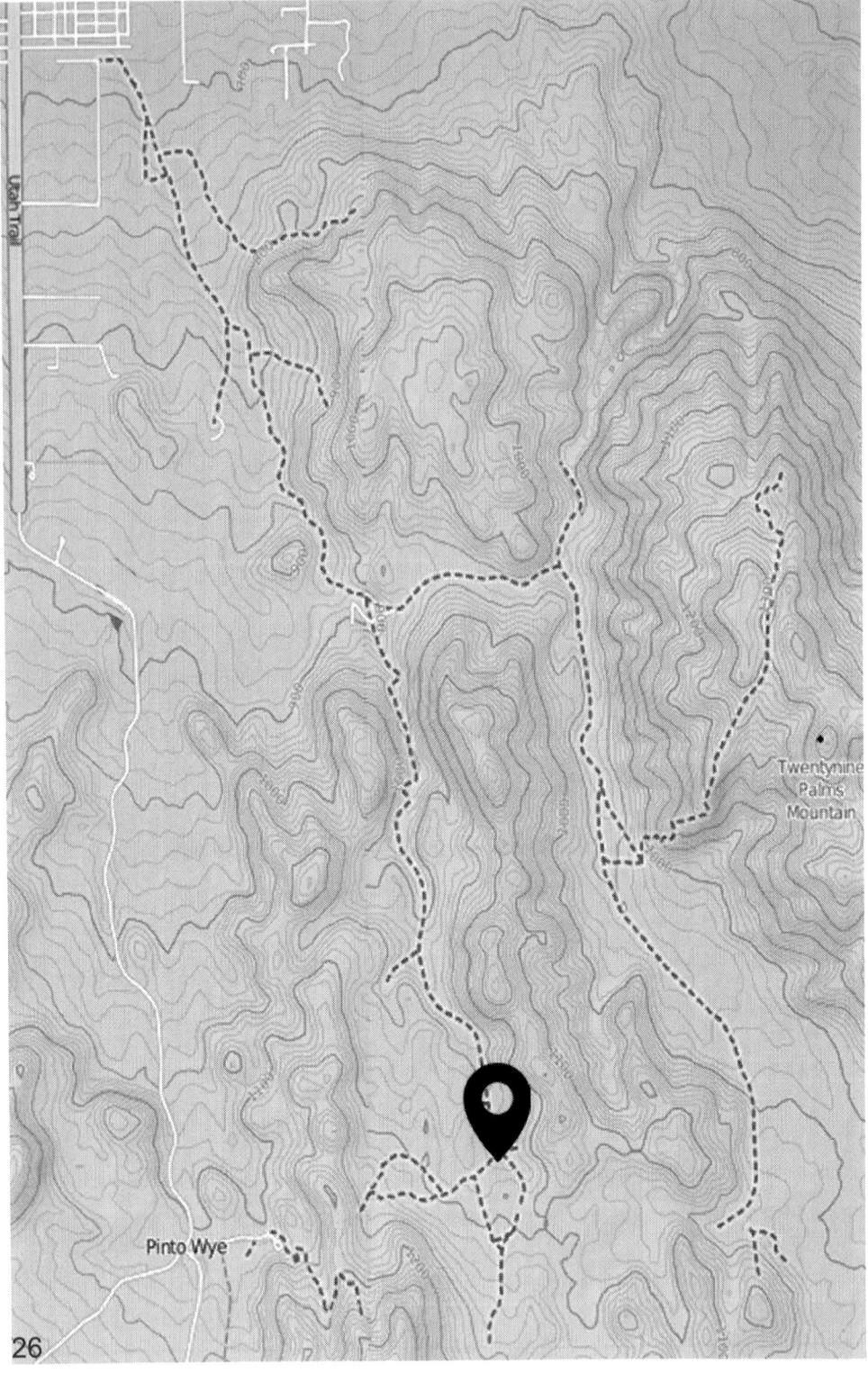

# Hensen Well

## GPS Coordinates: 33°5'37.90"N 116°6'30.22"W

Hensen Well was a small mining site located in the vicinity of Pushwalla Plateau, and Pleasant Valley. In possibly the late 1890's or early 1900's, a Chilean mill had been constructed on this site, as well as four stone structures, and a chimney.

A Chilean mill was used during the earliest days of gold mining, usually consisting of two large stones which rotated as it was pulled by a horse. The heavy stone would crush the ore, allowing one to see if the quartz was gold-bearing.

The Chilean mill at Hensen Well is no longer standing, but the large crushing wheels that had been used as part of the mill are still on site. Unlike the traditional stone wheels, the Hensen Mill utilized two iron wheels that had been filled with stones and concrete. You may have to look closely around the site to find the wheels, they are pretty well hidden by the thick vegetation.

The mill was a popular site for nearby mines (likely the Pinyon Mine, Hansen Mine and the Bonanza Lode) in the early 1900's to bring their ore to be crushed. When hiking the area many of the old miner roads are still visible in places, including the road leading to the Hensen Well Mill site.

Along with the stone structures, a lot of rusty gold remains, in the form of sardine cans, oil cans, canned goods, and broken glass bottles.

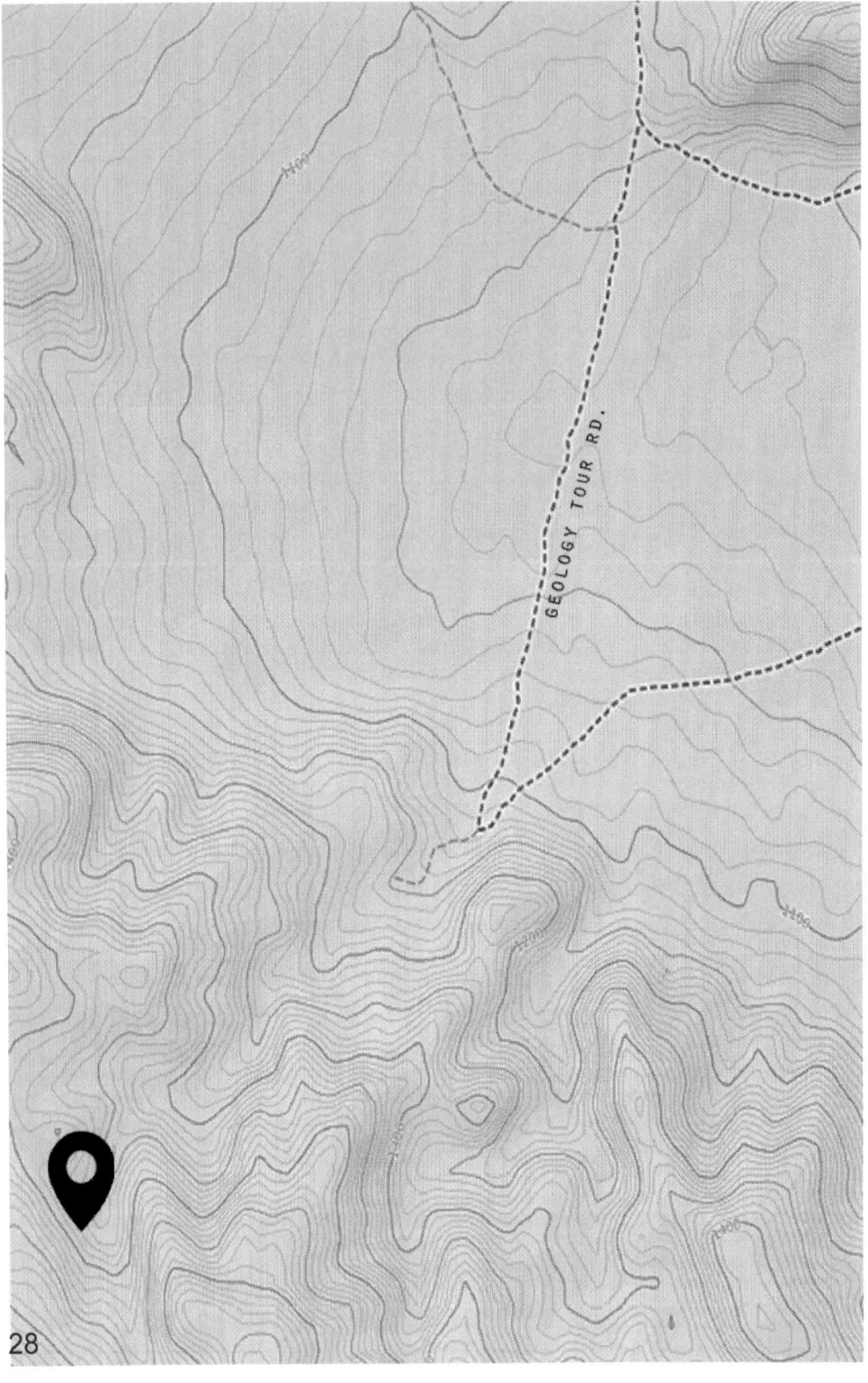

# Hexahedron Mine

## GPS Coordinates: 33°55'35.60"N 116°0'20.62"W

The Hexahedron Mine is located in the Hexi Mountains, it is accessible only by foot. The easiest route to get to the mine is to park at the Pleasant Valley Backcountry Board, and proceed east for roughly 2.5 miles. An old miners road runs along Fried Liver Wash, and is the easiest path to follow. The 2.5 mile hike takes you through a desolate portion of Pleasant Valley, very little plant life with the exception of creosote bush covers this part of the ancient dry lake.

As you are approaching the 2.5 mile point watch for an old road on the left, leading up into the Hexi Mountains. At this point you are in for the most difficult part of the trek. The hike up into the mountains is 1.7 miles with an elevation gain of over 800 feet. The road is rocky, and steep in places, nearly vertical for a short distance. From the road the views of the valley below are stunning.

Once you reach the mine there is a crumbling / roofless stone building. The stone building ruins are the highlight of the trip, the mines have been sealed by the Park Service, because as usual they have decided that it is their position to keep us safe from potential harm.

Historical data on the Hexahedron Mine is scant, but like most of the mines in the Hexi Mountains it was likely worked between 1900-1930.

The following more technical details regarding the mine are taken from California Journal of Mines and Geology, Volumes 12-13:

Hexahedron Mine (Quartz) – It is 7 miles N.E. of Pinon Mountain. The shoot of ore lies on the side of the hill. It is 75 ft. long, 15 to 20 ft. in thickness, and dips 45 degrees north. The ore occurs as a mineralization of a felsitic dike, which strikes nearly E. and W. At the west end it is small (not over 4 ft.), but widens in going east. It passes from the south to the north side of the range of hills in which it occurs, and at the where gold was found, lies exposed along the hillside, the overlying rocks having been eroded. Dikes of dark green diorite, much decomposed at the surface, have been thrust into the felsite and adjoining rocks in a very irregular manner, and in this vicinity the felsite contains gold. A small amount of iron oxide, copper carbonate, and dendritic infiltrations of mangangese oxide are the only indications suggesting ore. The most ordinary rock, having nothing in its appearance to suggest that it is gold-bearing, is seen on closer inspection to be spangled with small points of gold. In the vicinity of the Hexahedron Mine are some smaller prospects, on which a few holes have been sunk. Ed. Holland and A.G. Tingmas, of Indio, owners.

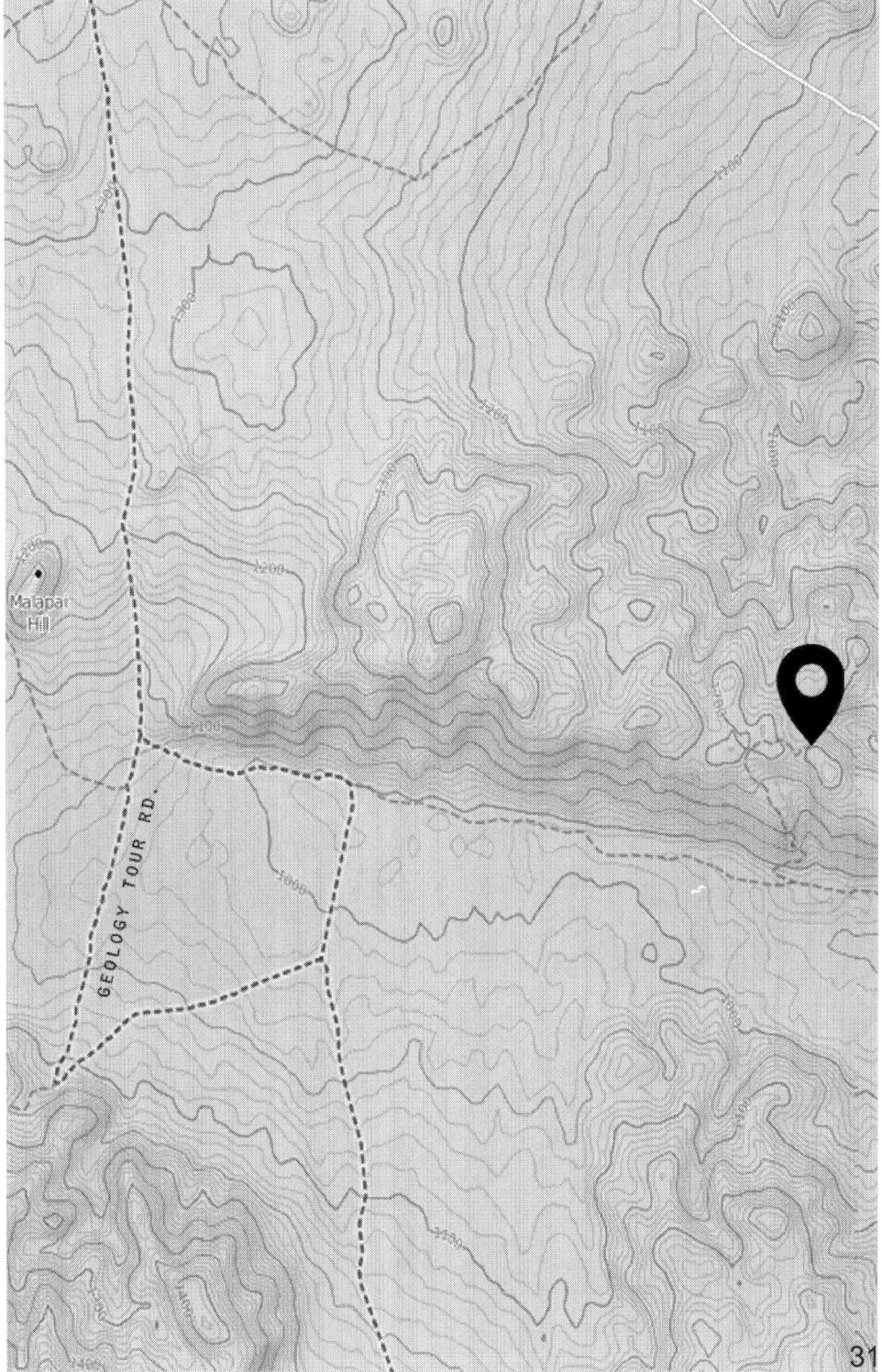

31

# "High Noon" Pictograph
## GPS Coordinates: 34° 1'54.80"N 116° 8'25.41"W

This is one of the more intriguing locations that I've had the opportunity to visit. Located in a wash near the Wonderland Ranch ruins, this giant granite boulder is hollow underneath. To view the pictographs you have to crawl through a hole, and once you are under the boulder there is enough room for a six-foot tall person to stand straight up.

The designs that are present are simple, yet interesting. Present are number of "ticks", which are believed by some to represent a calendar, or counting system. On the top, middle of the boulder is a pictograph of the sun. I speculate that the position of the sun pictograph indicates "high noon", which is why I have unofficially dubbed the site, "High Noon".

All of the designs that are present are made using a red pigment. One petroglyph is also present.

A blackened mortar hole is present above the entrance, likely used as a fire starting tool by the one time inhabitant.

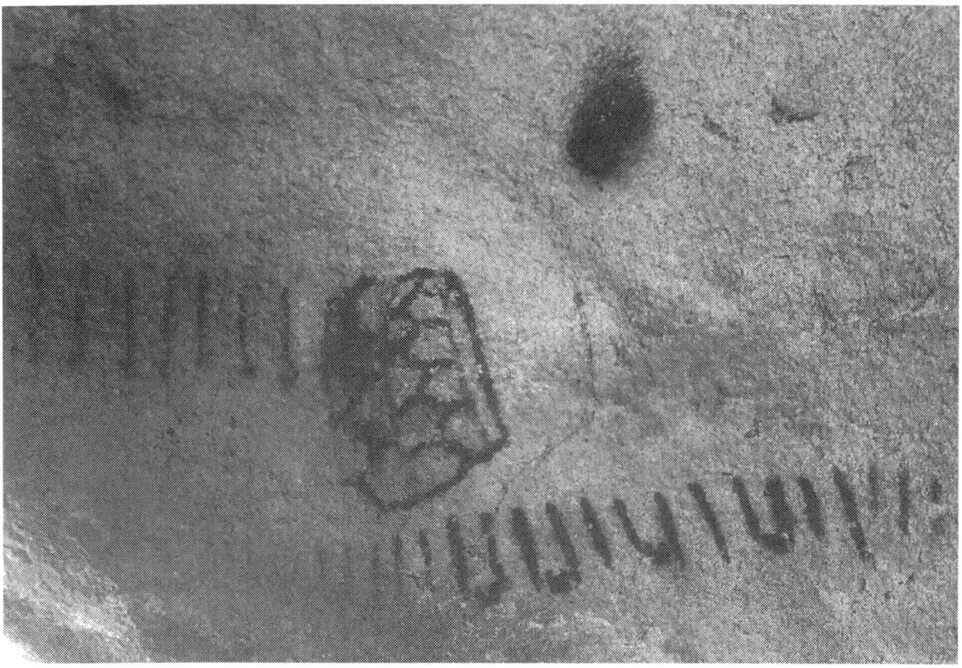

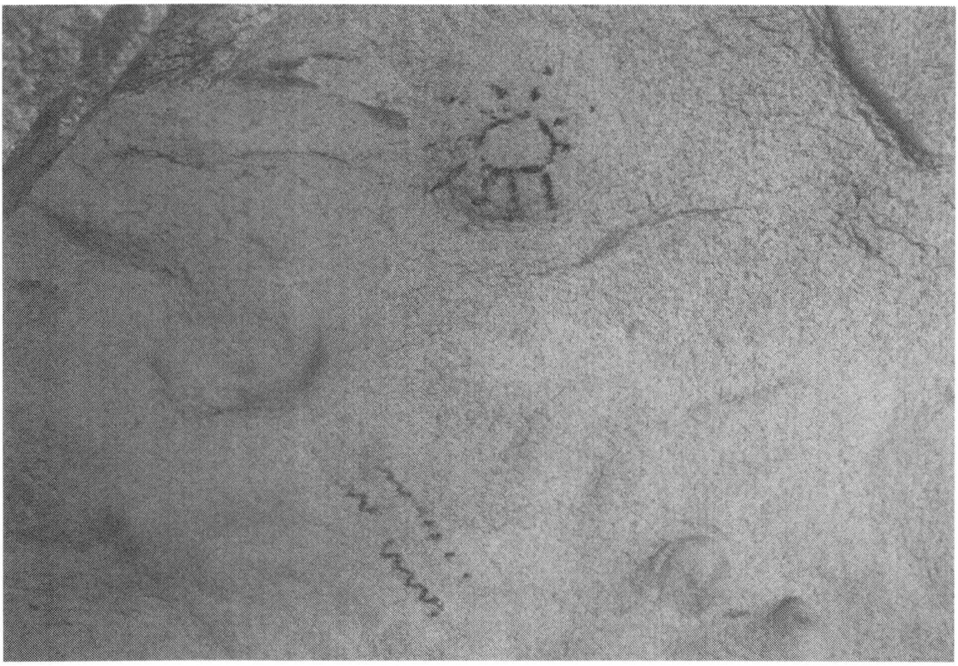

33

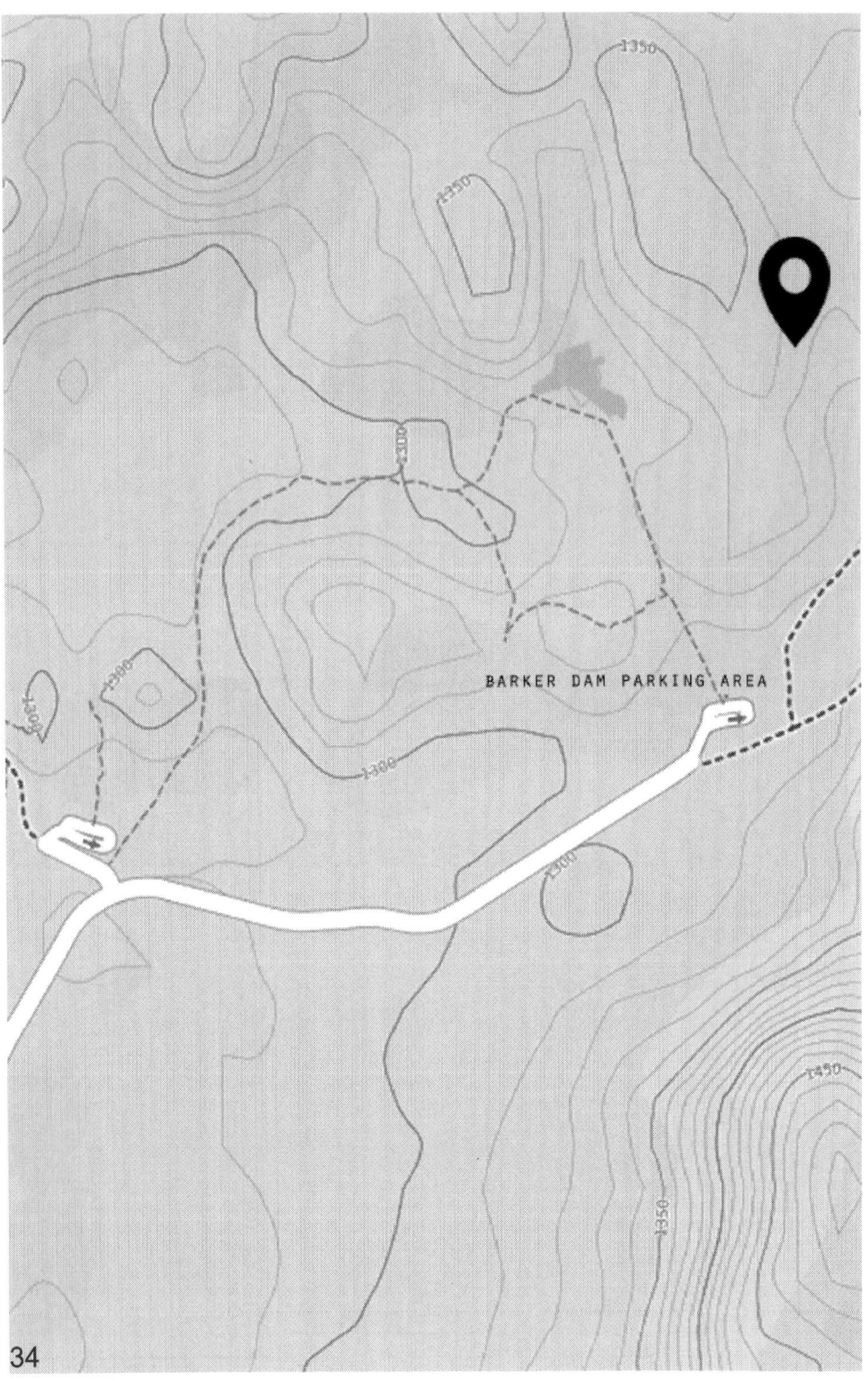

# Ivanhoe Mine

## GPS Coordinates: 34° 3'36.47"N 115°41'46.89"W

The Ivanhoe Mine is part of the Dale Mining District, outside of the town of Twentynine Palms, CA. Very little remains at the mine site today with the exception of a few concrete buildings slabs, and a small metal headframe.

For the underground explorer there is far more to explore below the surface. A report by the explorer group, The Underground Explorers, from March 2011 indicates that there are, "three levels filled with interesting artifacts, minerals, chutes and timbering." The group had descended on rope 270 feet, and was able to explore 95% of the Ivanhoe. As of my visit in July of 2013 the main tunnel appears to still be open, as well as numerous other cuts.

At the height of Ivanhoe's operation the quartz vein that they had worked, average 1 1/2 troy ounces of gold per ton.

The most exciting part of visiting the Ivanhoe Mine for us above ground types is the ride and the views. Ivanhoe Mine Road, while only a mile to the mine, climbs over 500 feet. The road is steep and rocky, but worth the drive. The views along the way are stellar, and only get better as you approach the mine (watch the above video for a short snippet of the drive to Ivanhoe Mine). Less than a quarter of a mile past the mine is a breathtaking lookout over Wonder Valley, which is nearly 2000 feet below.

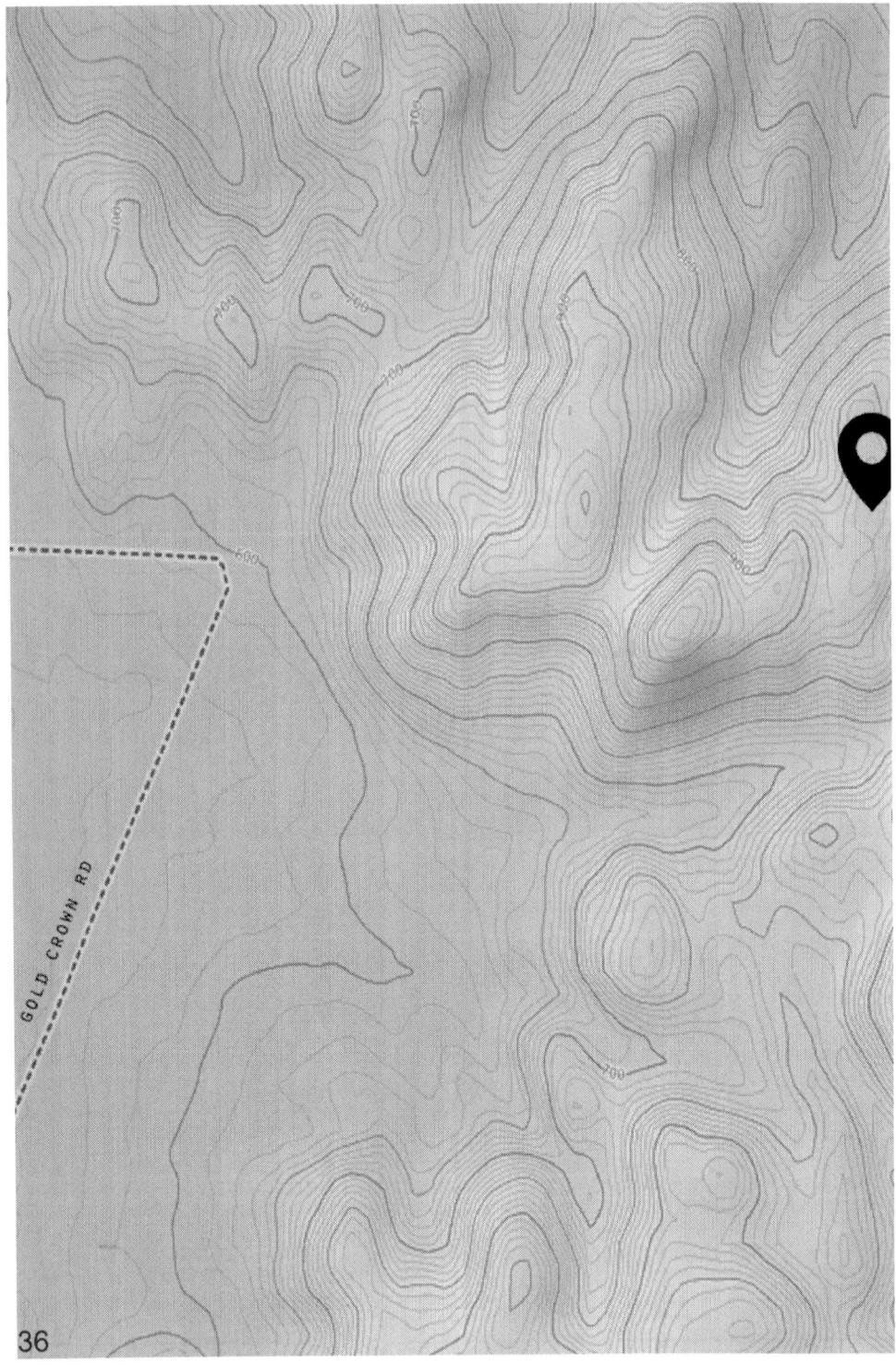

# O.K. Mine

## GPS Coordinates: 34° 2'44.82"N 115°42'16.43"W

The O.K. Mine was discovered in 1890 by John Burt. Burt and his partner F.J. Botsford worked the mine until 1899. In 1899 the mine was sold to the Seal of Gold Mining Company. The new ownership was able to sink larger dollars into the operation, and in turn was able to make the O.K. Mine one of the largest producing mines in the Dale Mining District. The production between the O.K. Mine and the nearby Supply Mine was so great that it prompted the entire town of Dale to pick up and move eight miles closer. They dubbed the new townsite New Dale.

The O.K. Mine had two 800 foot incline shafts, and featured a ten stamp mill.

One of the more interesting stories to come out of the O.K. Mine is about a mine worker named Charlie Thomas. Thomas was aware of the bi-weekly transportation between Dale and Amboy of roughly $18,000 in gold bullion. Thomas began plotting to perform a stick-up and make off with the bullion. He tried to enlist the help of some of his fellow miners, but none was interested.

On June 25, 1903, Thomas managed to collect three of the four guns that had been in town. The fourth gun belonged to Joe Wagner, a miner and town constable, his gun was kept under lock and key at the Dale Post Office. Wagner was out-of-town at the time, and when he returned he found roughly twenty men lined up along the outside of the post office, Thomas preparing to execute every one of them. Thomas

Thomas ordered Wagner into line along with the other twenty men. The first opportunity Wagner had, he jumped through the post office door, knocking it down, and retrieved his gun. Wagner shot Thomas dead on the spot. Thomas was buried in an unmarked grave.

Mining at the O.K. Mine has been on and off since its early days. The last larger scale operation that took place was in the 1980's. Total production is unknown.

There is a treasure tale about the O.K. Mine. The story is that Miklos Kovacs, a Hungarian prospect found a rich gold vein near the mines portal. Like most treasure tales, he was never able to relocate it. Treasure hunters today are still trying to find Kovacs rich gold vein.

A majority of the ruins of the O.K. Mine are from the late era mining that took place in the 1980's. A large headframe, with a deep vertical shaft is located roughly a quarter of a mile west of the main tunnels. Above the tunnels is a late era mill site, just in the last couple of years it has managed to be destroyed by vandals and likely metal thieves. An explosives bunker that was built into the mountain is located on the outskirts of the mine. The bunker is painted red, and features two foot thick concrete around the door.

Overall the O.K. Mine is an A-O.K. site to visit. Despite the vandalism the mine has more to see than a lot of the sites in Dale Mining District. A lot of what is left isn't very old, but it's a good glimpse of what a medium scale operation looked like in the 1980's.

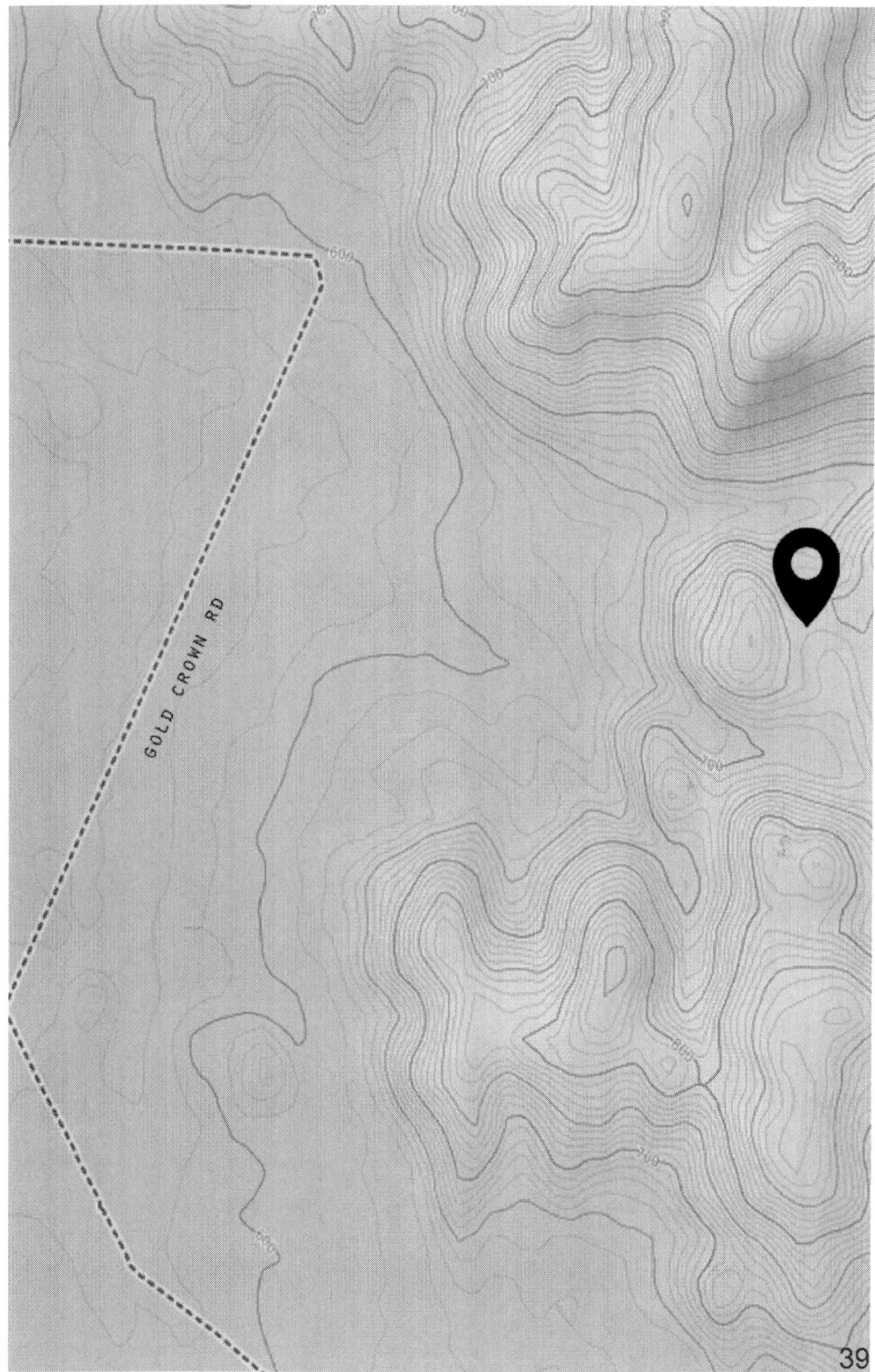

# Pleasant Valley Petroglyphs

## GPS Coordinates: 33°55'36.78"N 116° 4'31.00"W

The Pleasant Valley petroglyph site is small, consisting of roughly a dozen pecked images. They are located just a short distance from the site of the Serrano village of Squaw Tank. More than likely these petroglyphs were placed here during the time that the Serrano inhabiting the village site, placing these petroglyphs at around 1000 A.D..

The designs are mostly considered to be entoptic (created during a state of altered consciousness).

Some of the petroglyphs have been damaged in recent years by vandals, likely due to the close proximity of Geology Road, that leads through the valley.

# Queen Valley Pictograph

## GPS Coordinates: 34° 2'31.43"N 116° 5'30.14"W

The Queen Valley Pictograph Boulder sits at the base of the Queen Mountains. The area is semi-remote with only one dirt road accessing the most northern portion of the valley. At the base of the mountains there are a number of jumbo granite boulders like those in places more along the beaten path in Joshua Tree; various forms of cactus cover this trailess portion of the valley.

The number of hollowed out boulders, rock overhangs, and shelter/caves in the area made finding the boulder difficult, but with some tenacity I managed to track it down. The designs that are painted in the hollowed out rock face are in no way the Mona Lisa of rock art, they are simple lines and circles, likely documenting a part of the Native people's lives that once found shelter here.

There are a couple of things that stood out as unusual or odd about this particular site. A number of small dark stone knobs protrude from the shelter ceiling, each of these knobs contained a painted design on it. One of these designs is a sun, others appear to be X's, circles, and lines. The other unusual design that appears twice is an arrow pointing upward. One of these arrows is still clearly visible, the other requires image enhancement.

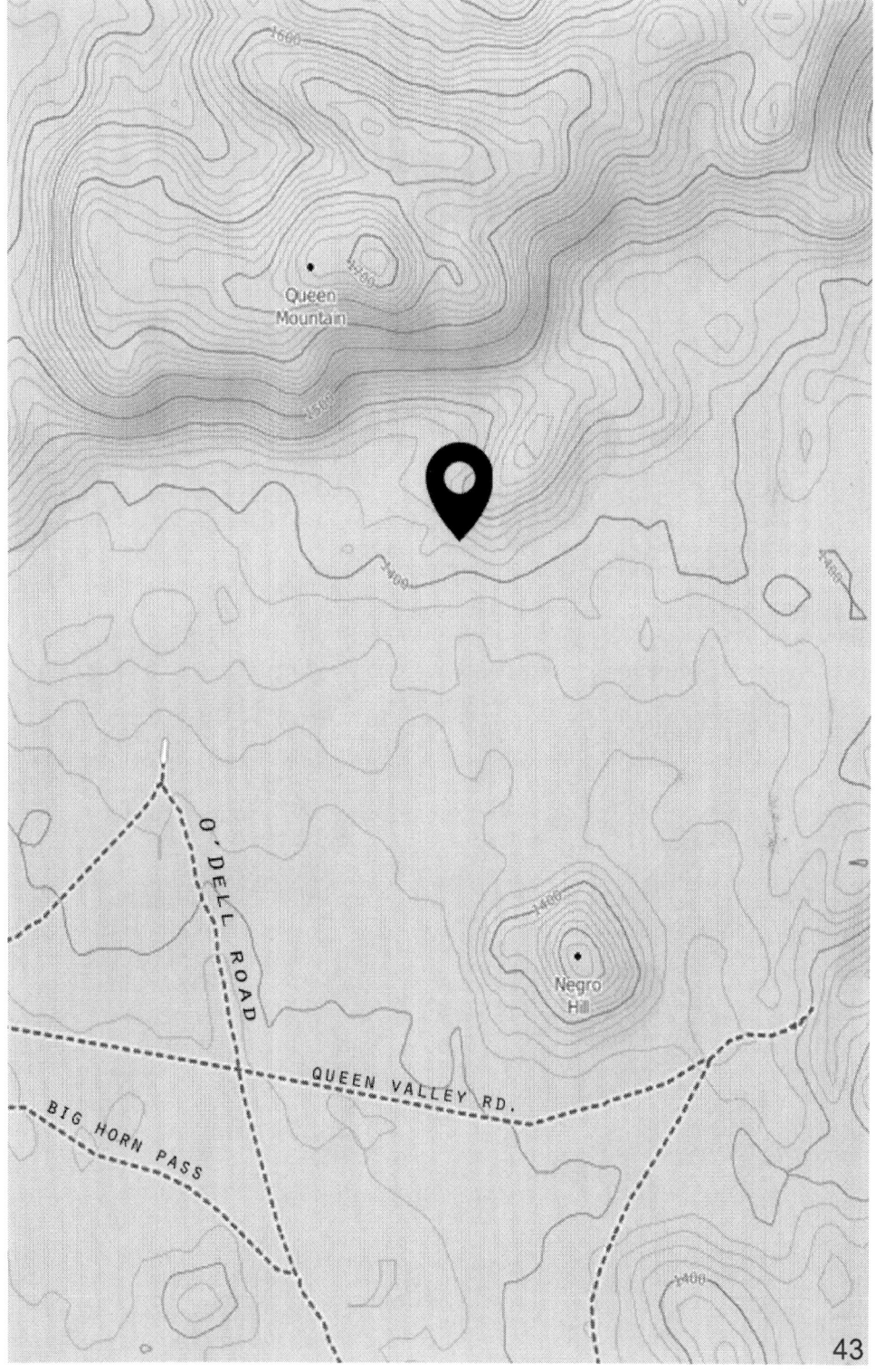

# Red Lady & Brunette Lady Pictographs

Red Lady Coordinates: 34° 1'36.18"N 116° 8'27.83"W
Brunette Lady: 34° 1'26.80"N 116° 9'19.00"W

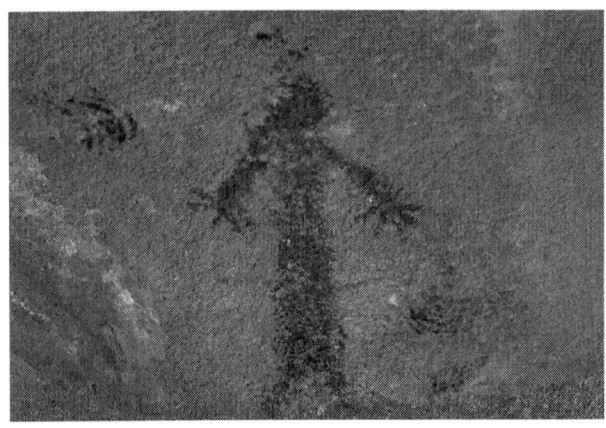

Both The Red Lady and Brunette Lady sites are believed to be Chemehuevi Indian sites, and are thought to indicate the first day of spring, also the beginning of the Chemehuevi's new calendar.

At the Brunette Lady site, researches have taken notice to that only on spring equinox, the sun can be seen through a notch at the site at sunrise. It is also thought that this site as well as the Red Lady site are fertility sites. Present at the Brunette Lady site, are what appear to be a set of twins. The twins may represent the 'twin sons of the sun', as told in the Chemehuevi legend of the "lone woman of the cave."

The Red Lady Pictograph site is located roughly a mile east of the Brunette Lady site. Like the Brunette Lady it is believed that this is a fertility site, and is tied to the "lone woman of the cave" story. The story indicates that a woman, "went out one morning to urinate and, as she spread her legs wide, the rising sun penetrated her with his rays and she became pregnant."

A large mortar hole is present at the Red Lady site. An archaeologist that has observed the site has documented on spring equinox, "One half hour before noon a small arrow shaped spot of light suddenly appeared, pointing to the bedrock mortar, the pointer grew in size, quickly moved toward the lone hole and then made a 'nose dive' into it." Reading into the ritual would indicate that the mortar hole acts as a vagina, and the arrow shaped rays of the sun, as a penis. When the sun rays enter the mortar, it is penetrating it, indicating a season of fertility.

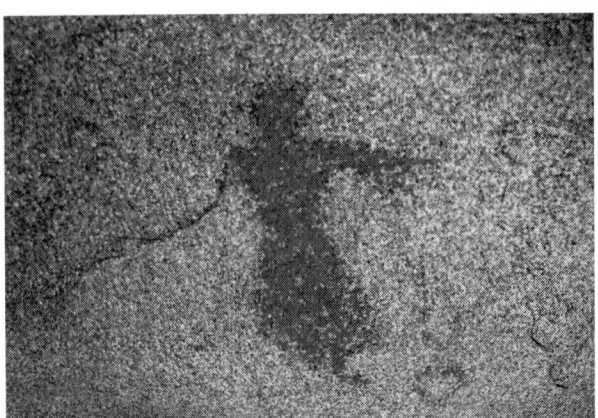

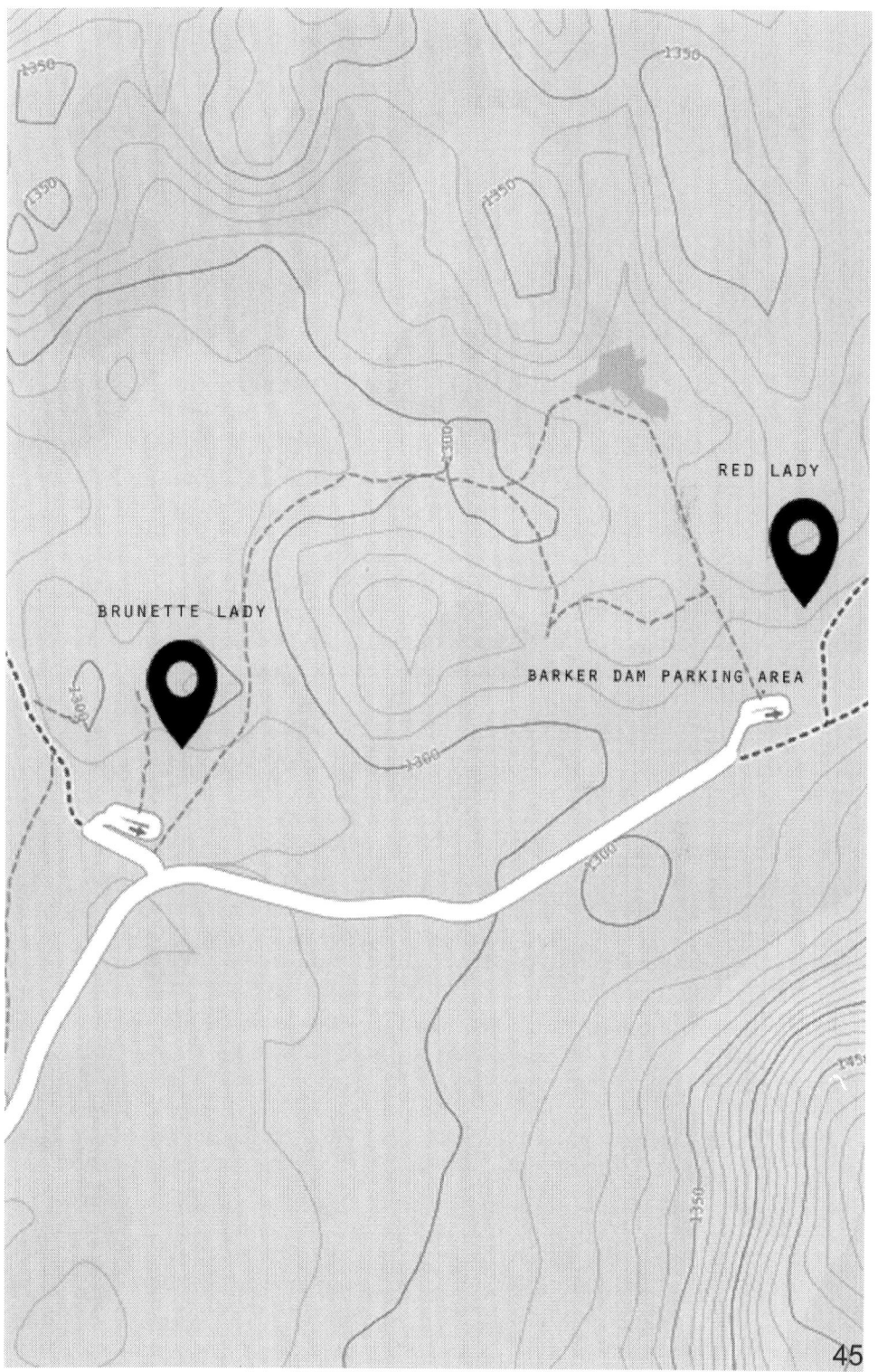

# Samuelson's Rocks

GPS Coordinates: 34° 2'52.09"N 116°14'34.26"W

John Samuelson was an area ranch hand and miner in the mid-1920's at the Key's Ranch. A citizen of Sweden, Samuelson claimed to have spent a majority of his life at sea.

In 1927, Samuelson decided to homestead his own piece of property in Lost Horse Valley, south of Quail Springs. He built his humble shack on top of a small hill, and mined his gold claims. In his spare time Samuelson carved eight political slogans, or rants rather on the boulders near his home.

After waiting out a year, Samuelson filed for his homestead in 1928, with the land office. Because of his Swedish citizenship, Samuelson was denied the ability to file his claim. This prompted Samuelson to sell his mining claims, and relocate himself and his wife to the Los Angeles area. Samuelson would kill two men at a dance hall in Compton a short year later.

Samuelson was arrested for the murders, but he never served time in prison. He was declared insane, and was hospitalized at California's State Hospital at Mendocino. He escaped a short time later.

In the 1950's, Samuelson resurfaced, working at a logging mill in Washington state. He died at the logging camp from an accident at the mill.

The house that Samuelson built-in Lost Horse Canyon burned down in the 1930's. The eight carved stones are all that remain of his time spent here. Interesting enough, the rants that he carved in stone 86 years ago are still relevant today.

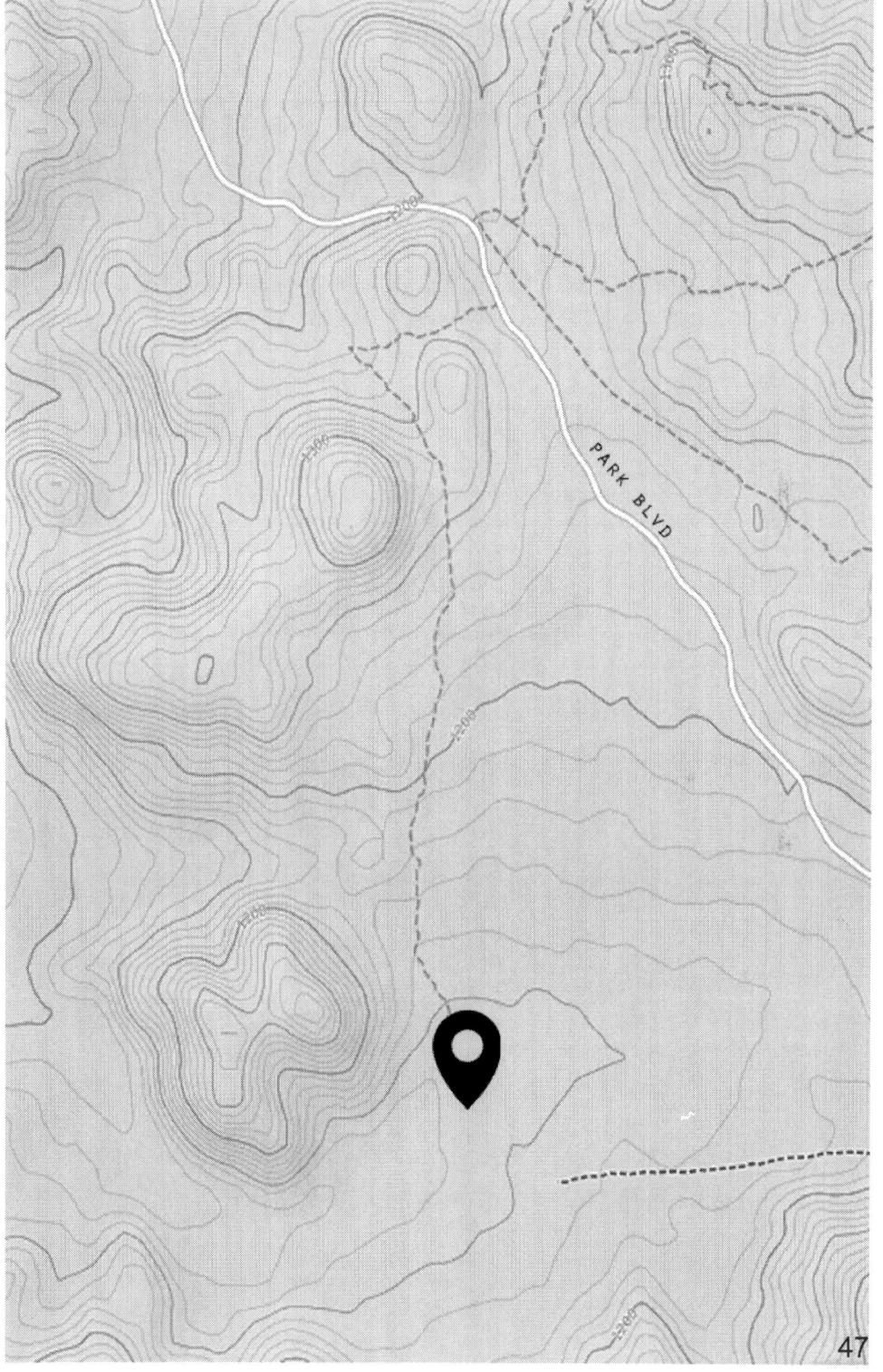

# Slab Rock Shelter Pictographs
## GPS Coordinates: 34° 1'42.61"N 116° 9'3.17"W

The Wonderland of Rocks area is a treasure trove of rock art sites, likely because of the water that regularly flowed through this area. Most of these sites remain little known to the general public, and the park service would like to keep it that way. All that it takes to locate these sites is a keen eye, and knowing the signs of what you are looking for. This particular site, I have called, "Slab Rock Shelter" due to the shelter's location above a large slab of granite.

The pictographs in the shelter consist of monochrome and polychrome designs. Three of the multiple red designs stand out the most and are visible without the use of enhancements. The polychrome designs use red and black pigments, they are more difficult to make out without enhancement. I have included both enhanced and unenhanced images in the gallery below to enable you to see the designs that are relatively invisible today.

Roughly 50 feet from the shelter there is a mortar hole. The mortar would have been used to grind nuts, berries and even small animals.

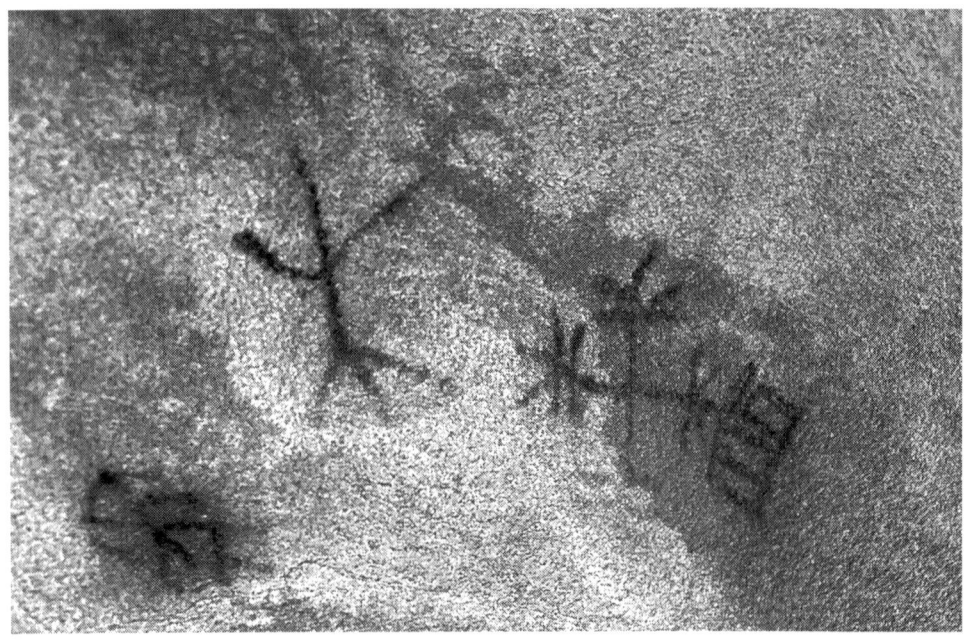

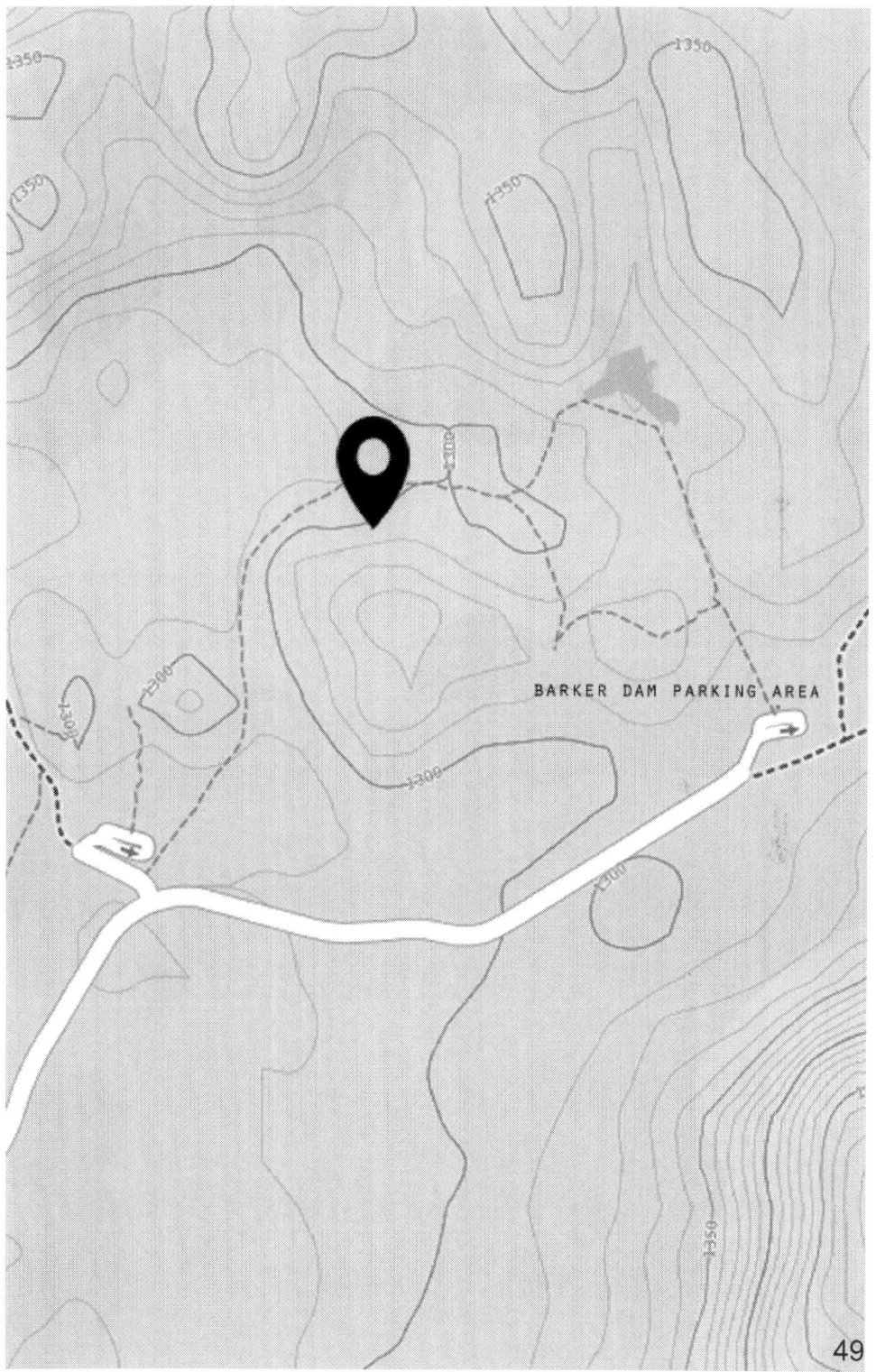

# Virginia Dale Mine

## GPS Coordinates: 34° 47.55"N 115°45'15.23"W

The Virginia Dale Mine and the Dale Mining District are located roughly 18 miles east of Twentynine Palms, and 8 miles north of Joshua Tree National Park. Virgina Dale is accessible via a 7.5 trip down Gold Crown Road from Highway 62. Gold Crown Road has a tendency to be sandy in places, so be mindful of this. The road leading up to Virginia Dale from Gold Crown is best hiked, there are places that soft sand is 6-8 inches deep and without the right equipment you'll likely find yourself stuck.

Placer gold was first discovered in the area in 1883 by Lew Curtis, by 1886 the Virgina Dale Mine was in full swing. Other mines in the area had already began producing not long after the initial discovery in 1883, near the town site of Dale (now referred to as Old Dale). Old Dale was located at the intersection of current day Highway 62 and Gold Crown Road meet.

The Virginia Dale Mine operated under The Virgina Dale Mining Company until 1899, when the company suspended operation. Despite the suspension of mining at Virginia Dale, the district continued to boom. After World War I, Virginia Dale was redeveloped by Jim Sigifus. Jim installed a new mill on the site, and attempted to sell the mine for half of a million dollar. Jim died before a deal could be struck. In 1923, Dave Post leased the mine, and three days into operation was shut down due to a lawsuit.

In the 1930s, a new life was given to Virgina Dale by a new operation that ran until 1937. It is estimated that during the operations peak, that 40 tons of ore was being extracted every day.

For 75 years, Virgina Dale has been in a state of abandonment. All the remains of the once bustling mine are Cyanide tanks, half standing stone walls, and foundations. Today the site is popular with recreational miners, and weekend desert warriors.

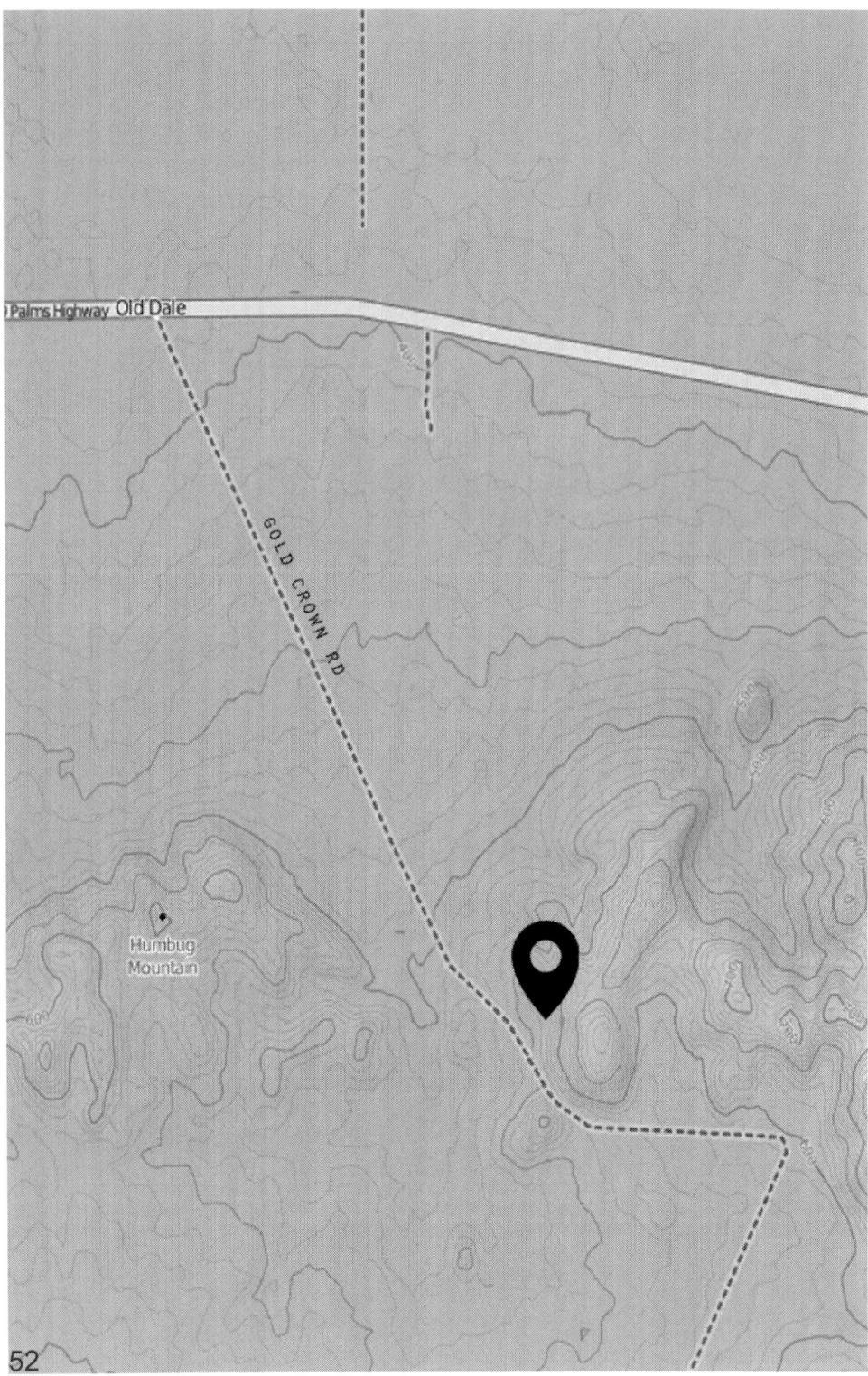

# Wall Street Mill

## GPS Coordinates: 34° 2'11.46"N 116° 8'2.44"W

The Wall Street Mill is located in the Wonderland of Rocks. It requires a short three-quarters of a mile hike from the Queen Valley Road parking area. The trail is well-defined and easy to follow. Along the trail you will pass a number of interesting historic ruins, from a large pink ranch building to old rusted out cars.

The story behind the Wall Street Mill has been confused many times over the years, and most sources that you might read have a number of inconsistencies and false information. I will try my best to piece together the story for you with the best possible sources of information that I have available.

Bill McHaney, a homesteader owned the property that the Wall Street Mill sits on. McHaney had acquired the land in 1896, and had dug a well there. Later a corral was built. The location became a popular cattle watering spot. Upon the death of McHaney; local prospector, homesteader, jack of all trade, Bill Keys made claim to the land.

Keys realized the potential of the location and its water source, and constructed the Wall Street Mill in 1932. A large majority of the mill had been previously in use at

Pinyon Well since 1891. Keys purchased the mill from the New Eldorado Company, he dismantled it and relocated it to its current location. Keys operated the Wall Street Mill as a custom mill, milling ore from other mines in the vicinity. It has been estimated that he may have milled for up to fifty different miners. The mill operated from 1932 until 1942 when the government shut down all unessential mines during World War II.

The mill was operated again briefly in 1949, and again in 1966. Upon the death of Keys, the National Park Service took over the site from the Keys estate.

The National Park Service has done a fantastic job preserving the mill, to this day it looks like Keys could return at any time to resume its operation. As little as a few years ago you could enter the mill buildings and get a good idea how the milling process worked, today the mill is fenced off and we are only left with being able to view the outer shell of the building. Never the less it is an impressive site that must be seen to fully appreciate.

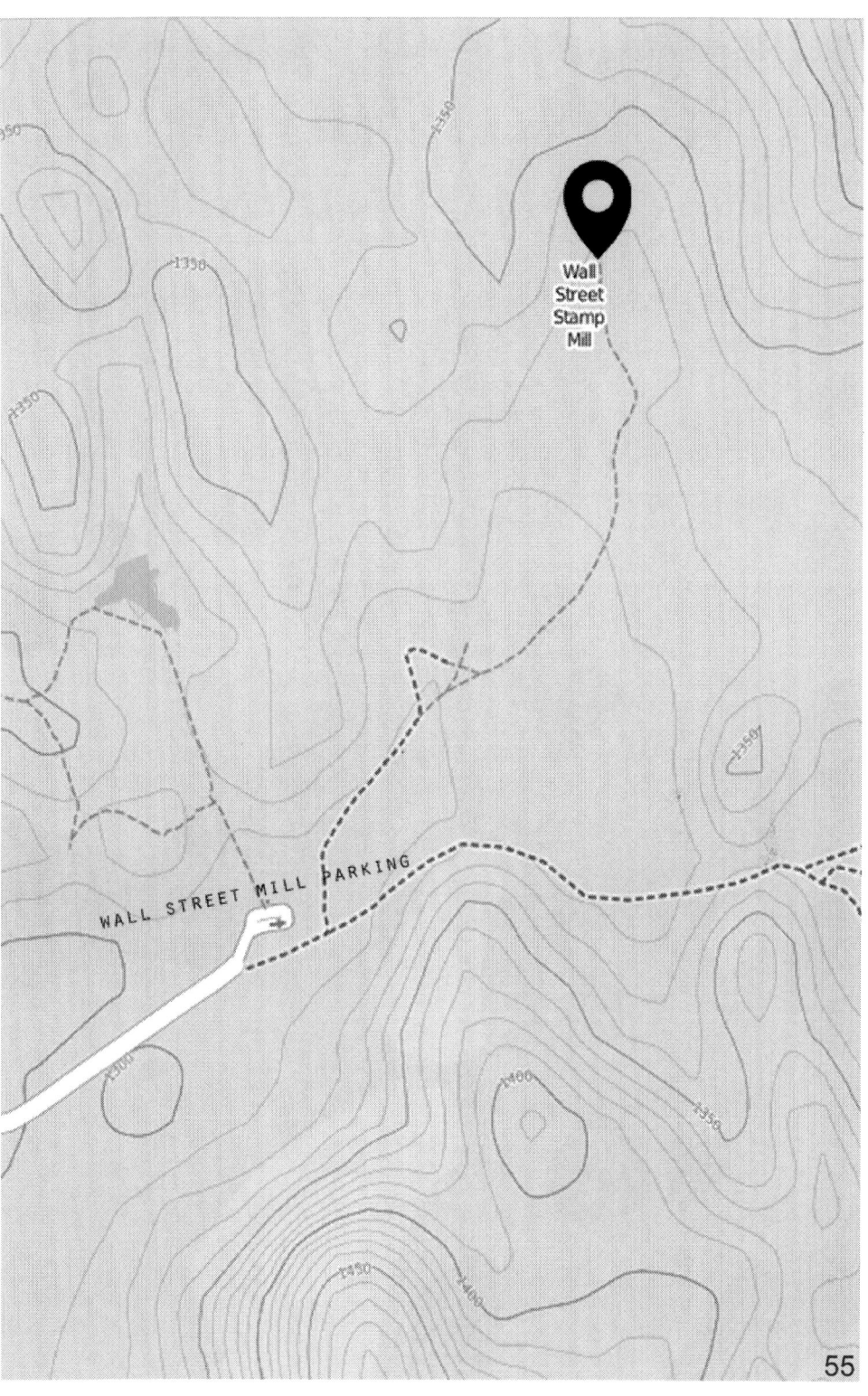

# Wonderland Ranch (Ohlson House)

## GPS Coordinates: 34° 1'49.08"N 116° 8'19.71"W

The Wonderland Ranch ruins are unusual and fascinating, the pink adobe structure sticks out like a sore thumb against the landscape.

Built by the Ohlson family, whom like many others came here on the search for gold; little else is know about the ranch and the family.

Today, many of the walls of the homestead have toppled over, however enough remains to allow you to paint a mental picture of what the house once looked like, as well as life on such a remote ranch in the early 1900's.

Over the years, visitors to the ranch have collected rusty, and glass treasures that they have found in the area, and have displayed them along the walls.

A concrete underground cistern, which was used to collect water for the ranch's use is collapsing, but still a rarity to see in these parts.

Up wash about 25 feet, hidden in thick vegetation is a cold storage compartment that was used to keep perishable items cool.

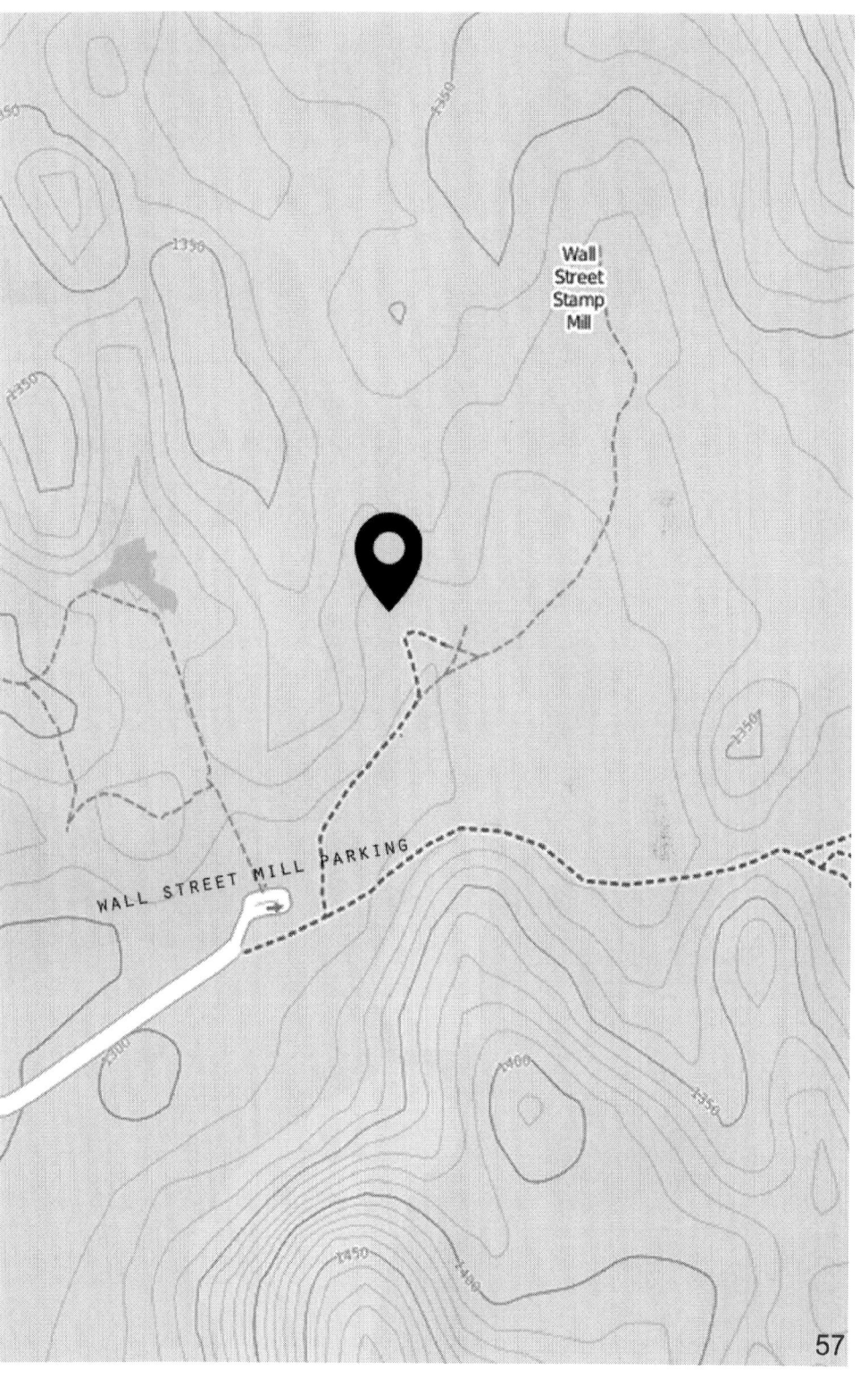

# Johnson & Lucerne Valleys

# Black Lava Butte Petroglyphs

GPS Coordinates: 34°14'15.83"N 116°29'40.09"W

The petroglyphs of Black Lava Butte have been largely overlooked as an important cultural site. The first field study performed here by archeologists took place in the late 1970's and early 1980's, since that time little study has been done.

In 2011, the ancient volcanic mesa was considered as the location of a future wind farm. The BLM fully aware of the sacred site that sat on top of the volcanic butte, issued a permit to Element Power, to install a 200-foot steel mast on Black Lava Butte. The steel mast was used to study the wind speeds prior to the installation of the turbine farm. Upon completion of their testing in 2012, Element Power announced that they would not be continuing the project because they did not believe the wind data collected is adequate for the kind of project development they were envisioning for the buttes.

There are no defined trails leading up, nor are there any trails on top of the 3-mile long, half-a-mile wide, mesa. It doesn't take long to begin stumbling upon some scattered petroglyphs, but the largest concentration is located at was once an ancient village or camp site.

At the camp/village site are at least 50 petroglyphs, mostly small abstract designs. They are difficult to spot because the basalt rock is scattered all over the ground, and the designs are faint from the aging process. Sleeping circles and grinding slicks are also prevalent, and make for further evidence of the likely camp/village site.

The most exciting find was a grinding slick that is roughly six foot by two foot in size. The rock is well-worn, and has a number of petroglyph designs carved in it; a grinding slick like this is truly a rare find.

Black Lava Butte was likely inhabited by the Chemehuevi Indians, however evidence of the Mohave Indians is also present. Late period Mohave Indian petroglyph designs consist of scratched lines, almost alway on top of older petroglyphs. These scratched lines are present at the village site.

While Black Lava Butte doesn't have hundreds of petroglyphs (as some reports have speculated), there are many unique designs and attributes to the site.

# Hondo Wash Rock Art Site

GPS Coordinates:     34°14'33.13"N 116°29'44.04"W

At Hondo Wash. there are at least five petroglyph panels. Some panels consisting of as few as one or two designs, and the larger panels consist of a maximum of ten designs. There are a number of sun symbols present at the various locations. One of the larger more obvious panels contains a few elements of modern graffiti, as well the year 1884 inscribed into it.

There are three pictograph panels, most of the elements are faded on these panels. The largest of the three panels contains some interesting elements that I have not come across previous to this location. Another of the panels has heavy smoke damage. Some small designs made from a red paint still manage to stand out despite a thick layer of black soot that covers them. The third panels consists of mostly finger prints, utilizing only the index finger, the middle finger, and the ring finger.

It is not clear the time frame this rock art was created, but it is likely that it had been painted and pecked by members of the Serrano Tribe that had occupied this area of the Mojave Desert for nearly 2,500 years.

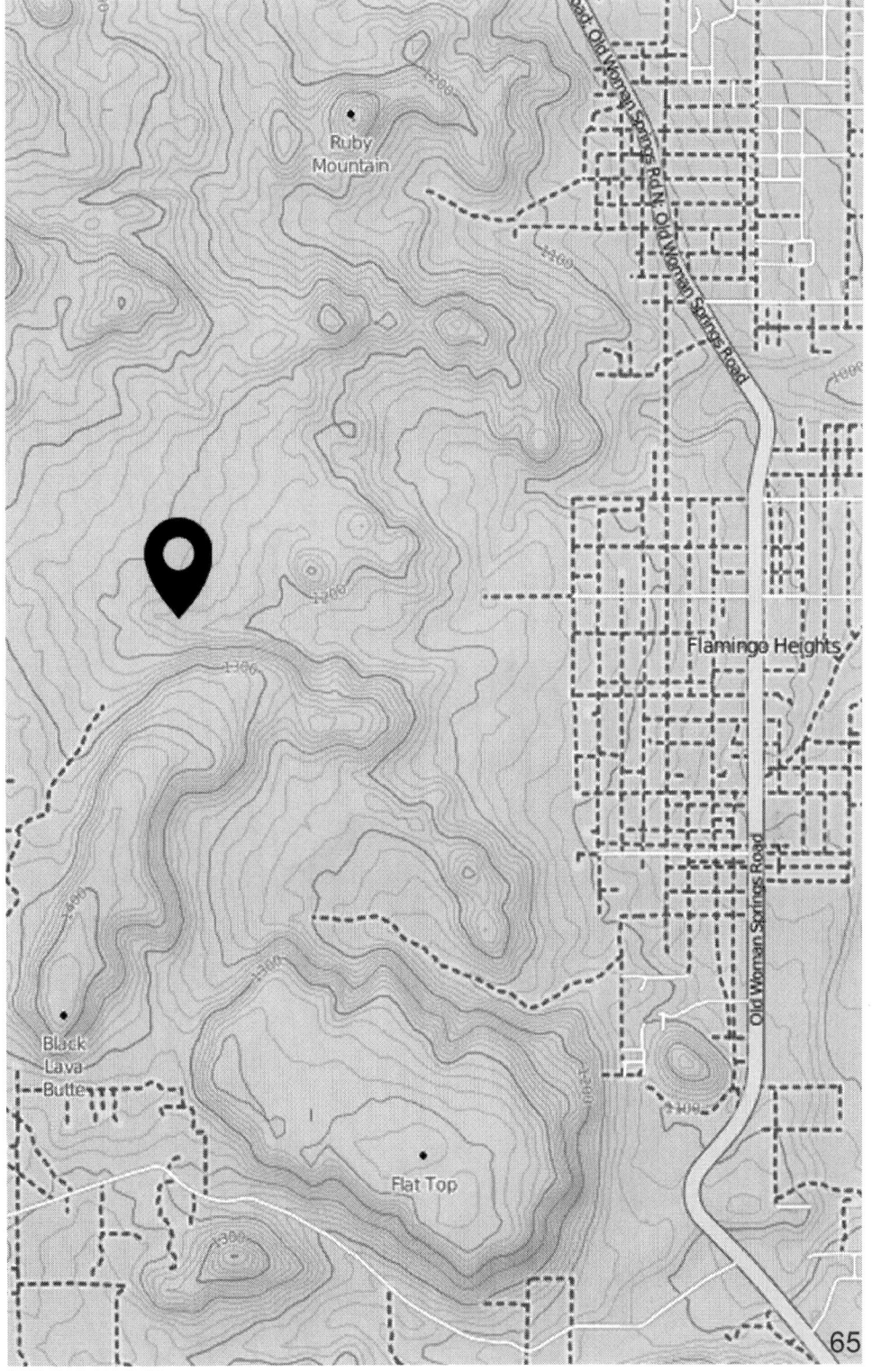

# King Clone Creosote Ring

## GPS Coordinates:   34°25'13.59"N 116°42'17.07"W

The Mojave Indians that settled this desert long before us white folks showed up, used the creosote as a medicine. The would make tea from the leaves. The tea would be used to treat colds, ease the pain of arthritis, and stop diarrhea.

In today's medical world the creosote plays an important role in fighting cancer, and can be used to treat AIDS as well as herpes.

Scientific research has indicated that the creosote bush is the oldest living organism on earth. This particular ring (looks more like a rectangle to me), known as King Clone Creosote Bush is the oldest known creosote in existence, at over 11,700 years old. This makes it older than the ancient bristlecone pine trees, and red wood trees.

While King Clone isn't the original plant that sprouted 11,700 or so years ago, each individual bush is a clone of the original, and continues to use the root system of that original creosote. As the current bushes die, they will again regrow using that original root system at a further distance away from the current plant, which expands the circle.

In the same area as the King Clone, there are additional creosote rings, but not near the diameter of the "King" itself.

# Lester Dale Mine

GPS Coordinates:   34°20'12.36"N 116°46'22.49"W

The housing complex at the Lester Dale Mine is a rare treat, with its still standing stone buildings and wooden ore shoot. The lack of historical documentation, however, frustrates me. I've scoured the internet, newspaper archives, and have even been in contact with the area Historical Society. I've come up empty-handed except for a few generic pieces of information.

The Lester Dale Mine overlooks Johnson Valley, from the northern slopes of the San Bernardino mountain range. Behind the mine sits the now-defunct Partin Limestone Quarry, which ceased operation in 2003.

I haven't been able to find the year in which mining began at the Lester Dale, but the few reports that I have managed to find indicate that the 1920s were the mines biggest production years. It is also thought that earlier Spanish settlers may have mined gold from this location, many years before white settlers made their way west. Other reports, however, indicate the Spanish never set foot in Johnson Valley due to its extreme remoteness.

The Lester Dale ceased operation in 1952.

Today we are left with the housing complex that once housed the miners and possibly their families. A larger building stands among the smaller stone buildings, likely a commons area that the miners shared, or possibly the headquarters building. The wooden roofs have long collapsed, but the stone buildings walls still have life in them.

# Rodman Mountain Grand Canyon

**GPS Coordinates:** 34°44'31.48"N 116°39'59.13"W

This box canyon in the Rodman Mountains was given the name the "Grand Canyon of the Rodmans" by none other than Bill "Shortfuse" Mann. Mann featured this site in his first book, "Guide to 50 Interesting and Mysterious Sites In The Mojave." I was in the area checking out some other lesser known locations, and decided to stop by and find out what Mann thought was so grand about this canyon.

A lot has changed at the "Grand Canyon of the Rodmans" since Mann first featured the site in his book in 1998, he described the canyon as, "There is a waterfall at the end of the canyon that has undercut the lava. In the sheltered spot is a beautiful, cool grotto that contains a small seep. There are many petroglyphs in the lava above the falls." Since Mann's writing the seep has dried up, and the petroglyphs seem to have disappeared (more on that in a moment). Mann goes on to say, "This is one of the most awesome and beautiful sites that I have ever seen in the desert and its relatively unknown." Upon arriving at the canyon I was met by four young men camping in the grotto, they had some pretty heavy artillery with them. It was obvious by the targets placed on the canyon walls that this once "awesome and beautiful site" was now a local favorite for target practice.

I asked the young men if they had seen the petroglyphs that Mann had mentioned. One of them told me that when he started coming here to shoot two years ago that there had been some petroglyphs on the dried up water fall, but they have all disappeared. He pointed out the location that they once where, and sure enough there was no trace of them to be found. I wanted to ask them if they thought that it was appropriate to be shooting at a cultural site, but didn't feel like stirring up problems with four armed men. Further evidence of vandalization in the form of spray painted rocks, fake petroglyphs, and random garbage is found in the canyon.

Another startling discovery is that the gas company ran underground pipelines throughout the area. The scares are evident for miles around, and a portion of the box canyon was destroyed in the process.

If Mann was still alive today, he surely wouldn't find his "Grand Canyon of the Rodmans", to be so grand. While still a beautiful site when you look past the obvious mistreatment that the canyon has had in recent years, it just isn't what it sounds like it used to be.

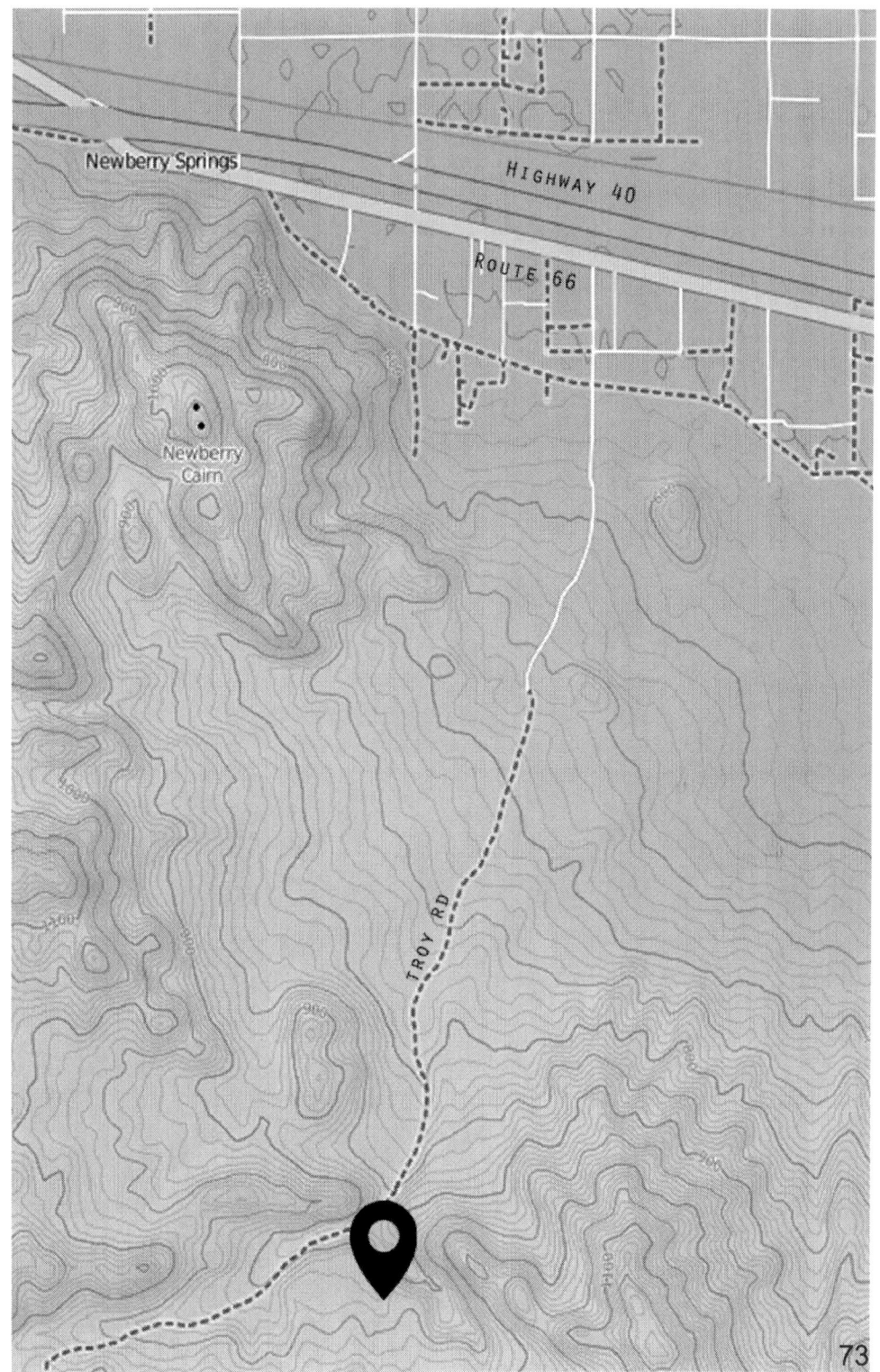

# Spanish Smelter

## GPS Coordinates: 34°13'35.95"N 116°40'21.69"W

Located at an elevation of 6,161 feet, in the San Bernardino Mountains, the easiest access is via Forest Service Route 2N02 (Burns Canyon Rd.). Where 2N02 intersects with 2N61Y, turn on 2N61Y. Follow 2N61Y for .16 mile. Park in the wash, and walk south-west down the wash for one tenth of a mile. The smelter will be on your left, and the ruins of a stone cabin on your right.

The smelter is speculated to have been built in the early to mid 1800's by Spanish miners. The Spanish was the earliest known people to have mined in the San Bernardino Mountains, their earliest exploration of this region goes back to the 1770's.

A deposit of Cinnabar (Mercury), is located near the site of the smelter. It is likely that the smelter was used to recover the mercury. The mercury was then used to recover fine gold.

The smelter is in impeccable condition for its age, you can almost image the miners returning at any moment to fire it back up.

As with any historic landmark, enjoy it, but don't disturb it. This smelter has likely survived for nearly 200 years, and without our interference it will hopefully stand the test of time.

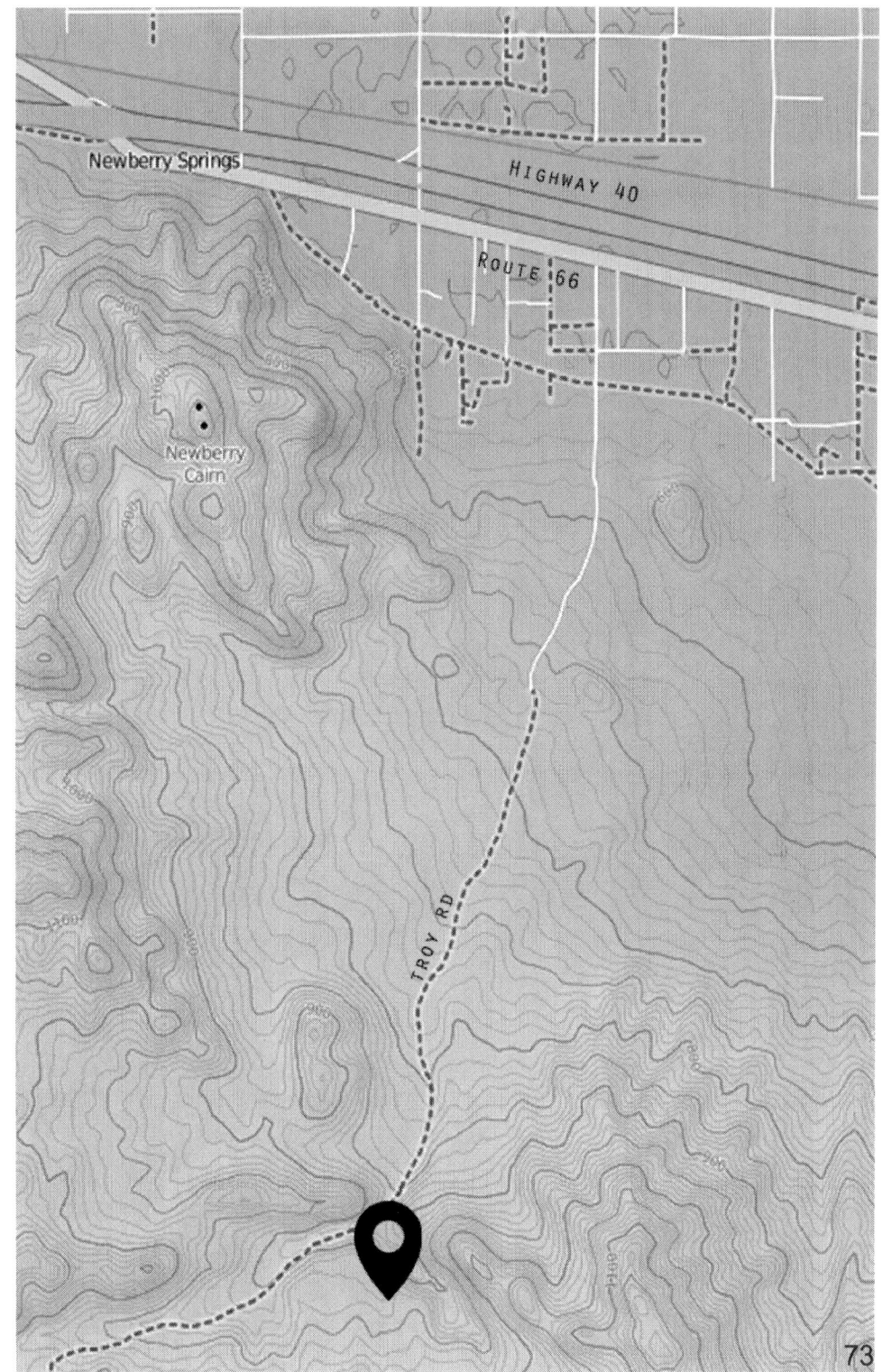

73

# Spanish Smelter

## GPS Coordinates: 34°13'35.95"N 116°40'21.69"W

Located at an elevation of 6,161 feet, in the San Bernardino Mountains, the easiest access is via Forest Service Route 2N02 (Burns Canyon Rd.). Where 2N02 intersects with 2N61Y, turn on 2N61Y. Follow 2N61Y for .16 mile. Park in the wash, and walk south-west down the wash for one tenth of a mile. The smelter will be on your left, and the ruins of a stone cabin on your right.

The smelter is speculated to have been built in the early to mid 1800's by Spanish miners. The Spanish was the earliest known people to have mined in the San Bernardino Mountains, their earliest exploration of this region goes back to the 1770's.

A deposit of Cinnabar (Mercury), is located near the site of the smelter. It is likely that the smelter was used to recover the mercury. The mercury was then used to recover fine gold.

The smelter is in impeccable condition for its age, you can almost image the miners returning at any moment to fire it back up.

As with any historic landmark, enjoy it, but don't disturb it. This smelter has likely survived for nearly 200 years, and without our interference it will hopefully stand the test of time.

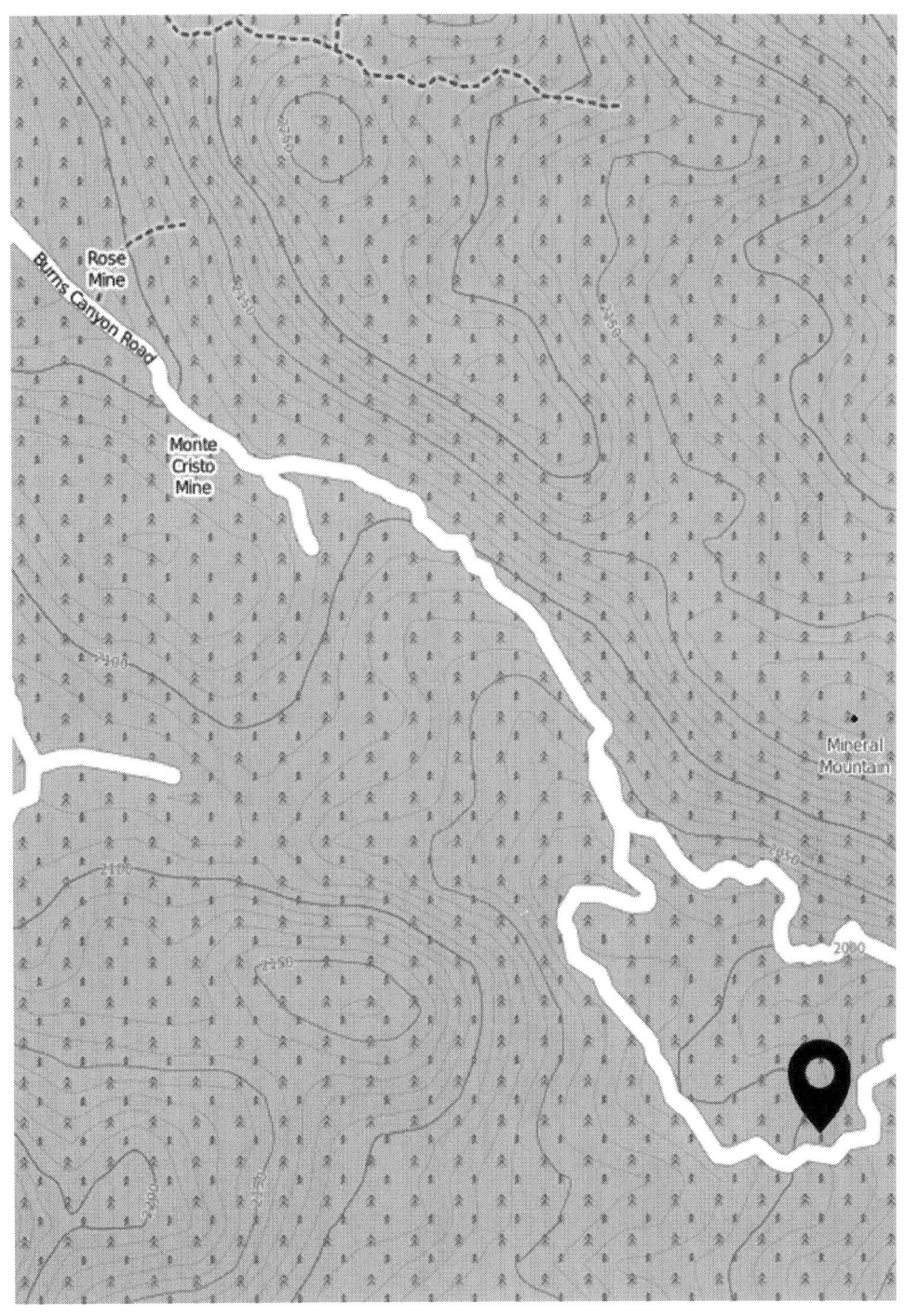

# Viscera Spring / Vaughn Spring

## GPS Coordinates: 34°15'45.56"N 116°39'31.57"W

Nestled in the San Bernardino Mountains, roughly fifteen miles due east of Big Bear Lake, is a small abandoned community that was built around three area springs, Viscera Spring, Vaughn Spring, and Mound Spring. It is a semi-arid environment, with Joshua Trees, Pinyon Pines, Manzanita and other brush. The homes, cabins and ranches that made up this community are spread out over an area of a little over a mile.

A number of gold mines are within the vicinity, including the Bighorn Mine. In 2010, the National Forest Service is known to have removed a number of historic miner cabins from this same general area. It is unclear, if any of the remaining abandoned structures belonged to any of the miners, or if they are from people settled the area after the mines had closed. Some of the structures appear to not be as old as others, while another look to have been a family ranch.

Some of the structures are signed no trespassing, while others are not. Please respect these signs, and stay out of the buildings that are clearly marked. The ones that are not signed, you are more than likely safe to use for camping and shelter. Sadly most of these structures have seen better days, years of abandonment and their remote location have made them a target for vandals.

# Yaranka Canyon Petroglyphs

## GPS Coordinates: 34°19'47.21"N 116°32'10.63"W

There are four panels to the Yaranka Canyon site. The designs are abstract and mostly geometric shapes. There is an obvious sun design on one of the panels. A faint diamond chain pattern can be made out on another. The diamond chain pattern may represent a girl entering puberty, thus possibly making this a puberty site.

Native people arrived in Johnson Valley an estimated 11,000 years ago. The last known Native inhabitants were the Serranos. The Serranos stayed in Johnson Valley for a short period, and left the valley in the 1870's because epidemics began to kill off the tribe.

Some modern graffiti is located at the site, near the petroglyphs. Thankfully it appear that the vandals didn't actually paint any graffiti on top of the ancient designs, but rather directly beside them. This doesn't excuse the fact that a cultural site was vandalized, it just means that the idiot that performed the task wasn't as big of an idiot as they could have been.

Nearby there is a small crumbling rock cabin against a granite boulder outcropping. At this cabin there are two additional petroglyphs. One of which is a female figure. The design is similar to female petroglyph symbols in the Barker Dam area of Joshua Tree National Park.

# The Mojave National Preserve

# Bert Smith Rock Cabin

## GPS Coordinates: 35° 9'14.94"N 115°20'1.86"W

Bert George Smith, was a World War I veteran, he had suffered the effects of shell shock and was a victim of poison gas. The Bureau of Veterans Affairs sent him to live in the desert, with the hopes that he would live a longer life, due to the climate.

Smith built this cabin in 1929, originally a wood framed building, he added the stone in later years. Despite his short life expectancy, Smith lived at this cabin at Rock Springs until the mid-1950s. He died in 1967, at a rest home.

The stone cabin has been restored both inside and out by the National Park Service. There is no access to the inside of the cabin, yet you can view the inside through the windows.

There is a small picnic area and pit toilets near the cabin, and a hiking trail leads from behind the cabin to lower Rock Springs.

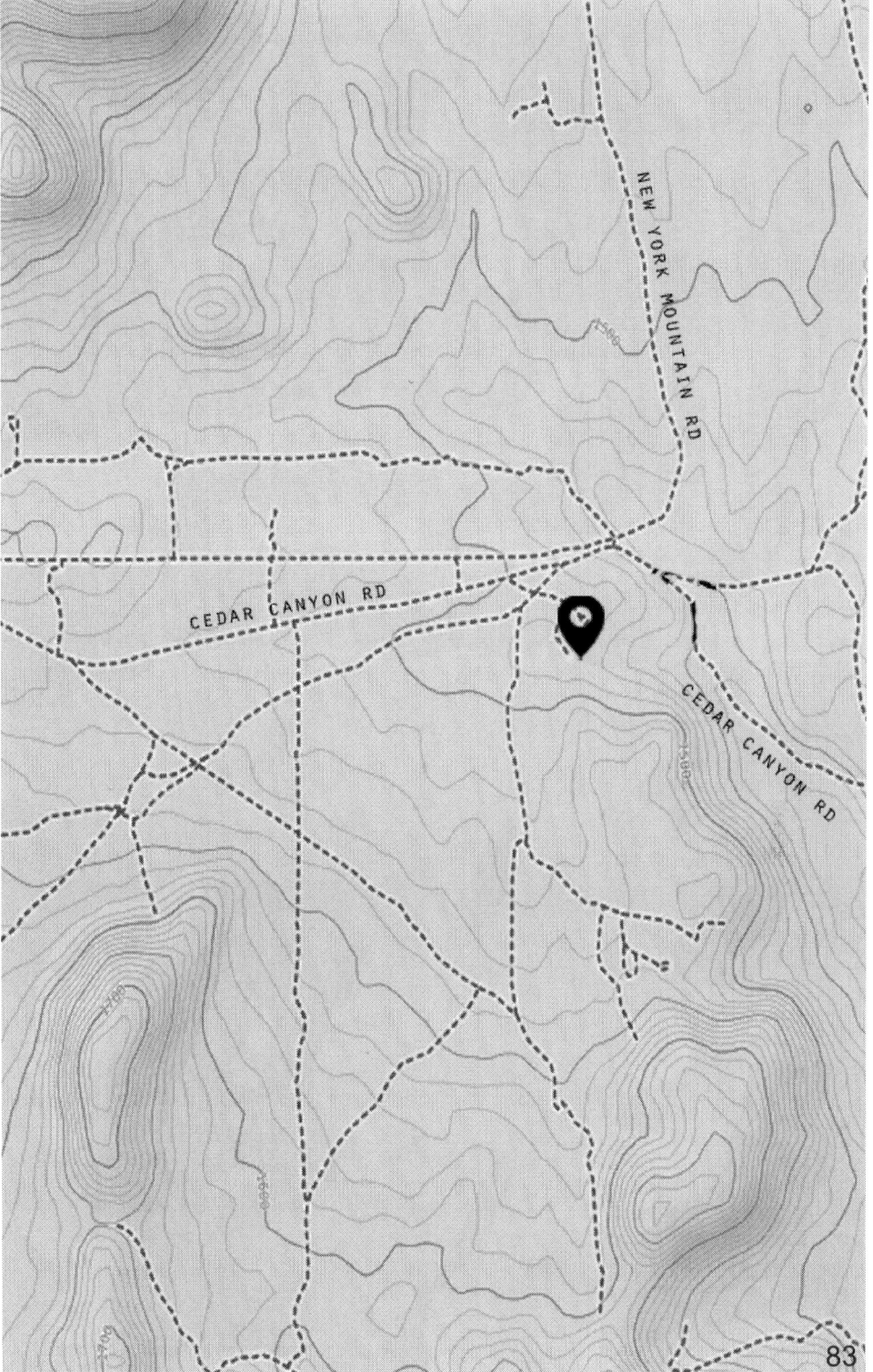

# Big Horn Mine

## GPS Coordinates: 34°50'28.07"N 115°32'32.14"W

The Big Horn Mine is located on the east side of the Providence Mountain Range. Gold was first discovered here in 1894, a dozen or so claims were filed. Originally named after the Mable, Contention, and Investment mines. Thomas Gannon and his partner Barker, were the first to develop any of the claims. In 1898, they sunk a 200 foot shaft at the Contention claim. They managed to expose a wide ore bearing ledge that just got richer the further down in-depth it went.

Gannon managed to work the mines here for nearly 30 years. Estimates have been made based on reports from outside sources that from late 1918 – early 1919, he managed to produce $100,000 worth of ore. Apparently enough money for Gannon to stop production from 1920-1924. Upon his return in 1924 he worked the Contention and Subway shafts. It is not known how much ore was processed, but in the tailings alone there was 6,000 tons worth an estimated $30,000.

In the 1930's the mine was sold, but it laid idle until the late 1930s. The Big Horn Exploration Company purchased, renamed the mine, and began working the site. Big Horn Exploration meant business, and sunk deeper shafts in the already present Contention and Subways shafts. They also built an 80-foot headframe, with ore bins and a hoist. The Big Horn Exploration Company operated the mine until 1943, when the mine was closed for good.

The Hilltop House which was built prior to 1933 is an impressive site that is still standing today. The building was the residence of W.E. Wilson, the Bighorn Mine operator as well as primary investors Herbert and Anna von Wagenheim. The house was also a welcoming place to area miners, ranchers and homesteaders during the holidays for celebrations.

The House was in poor shape leading up to 2008, and due to high winds the building finally collapsed. The park service restored the building that same year thanks to a grant from the Vanishing Treasures fund. Today the building stands proudly as a piece of early mining history.

The old mining site is filled with other treasures as well, including numerous water tanks, stone building ruins, and old rusted cars and equipment. The mines have been sealed, so underground exploring is not possible at this location.

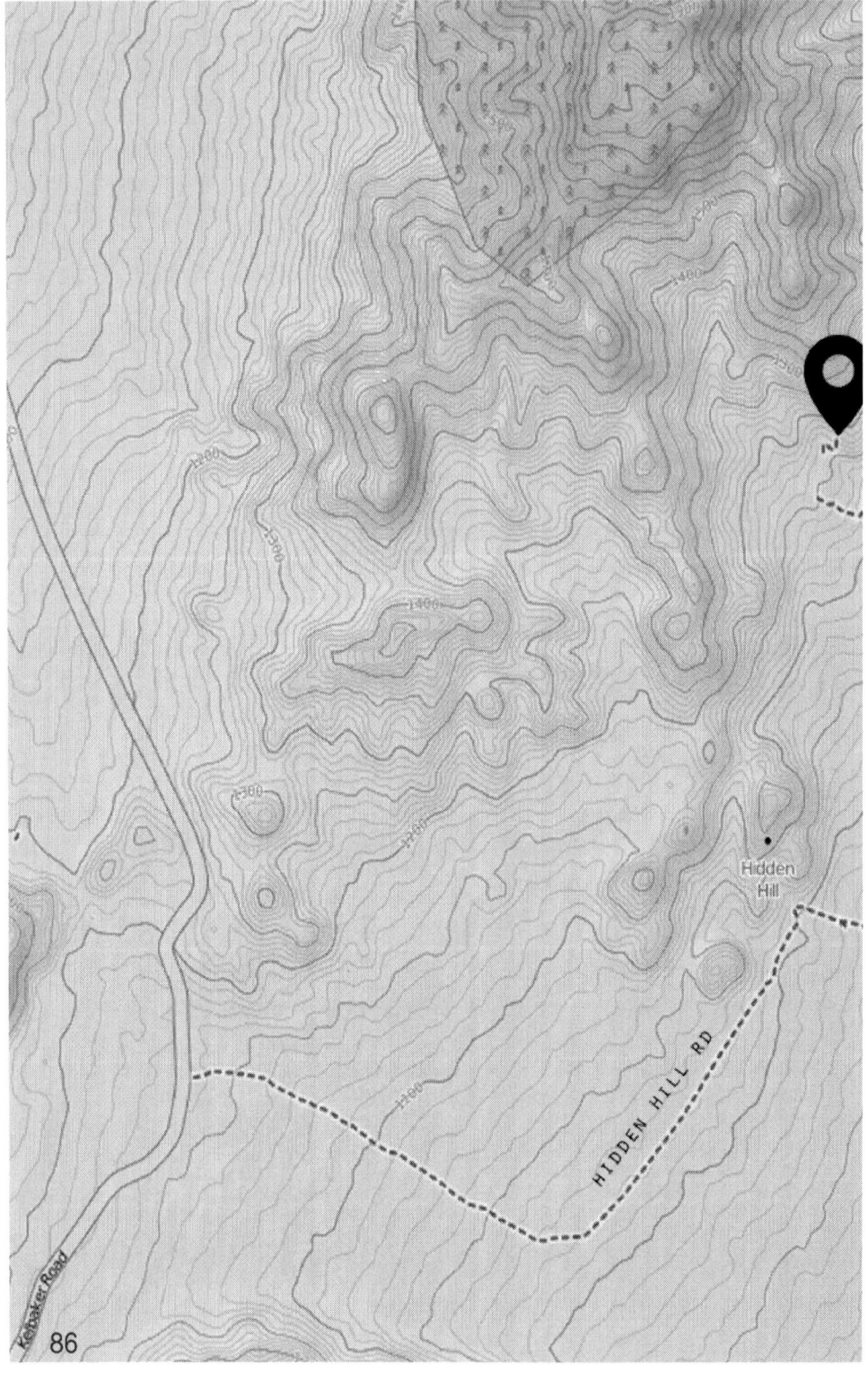

# Black Tank Wash Petroglyphs
# Aiken Arch Pictographs

Black Tank Wash Coord: 35°14'29.96"N 115°44'48.52"W
Aiken Arch Coordinates: 35°14'26.53"N 115°44'52.12"W

Black Tank Wash is situated in the Aiken Cinder Cone field, in the northwest section of the Mojave National Preserve. It runs southwest, for roughly 12-miles, through the Cinder Cone field. The wash lies between ten to twenty-foot vertical basalt walls. The setting is picturesque, with black lava beds, and cinder cones surrounding the area. The area is mostly wilderness, with Aiken Mine Road, being the only vehicular access to the heart of the wilderness.

The cinder cones are essentially "little" volcanos. Researchers believe that they began erupting 7.6 million years ago. The last lava flow being as recent as 10,000 years ago. The Aiken Cinder Cone field was made, Cinder Cone National Natural Landmark, in 1973.

Aiken Arch, a natural arch, which is located in Black Tank Wash was formed by the lava flow thousands of years ago. Under the arch, there are both red and white (red is the dominating color) pictographs, mostly geometric designs, but some anthropo

morphs. Some of the pictographs are still vibrant even after having been in the elements for possibly hundreds or thousands of years.

For roughly a half mile, in either direction of the arch, along the basalt walls, are hundreds of petroglyphs. The petroglyphs have been identified as being from both Archaic times (the second period of human occupation in the Americas, from around 8000 to 2000 BC), as well as more recent Numic (Native American ancestors of the Ute, Paiute and Shoshone, who are thought to have moved into the Great Basin of the United States from California about AD 1000).

The Native people were likely attracted to this particular location, because of the natural arch. Many Native cultures around the world view a natural rock arch, as a source of numinous power. The petroglyphs and pictographs that have been created here, may very well tell the stories of this power. Or possibly they had been placed here to invoke that power. We will likely never know.

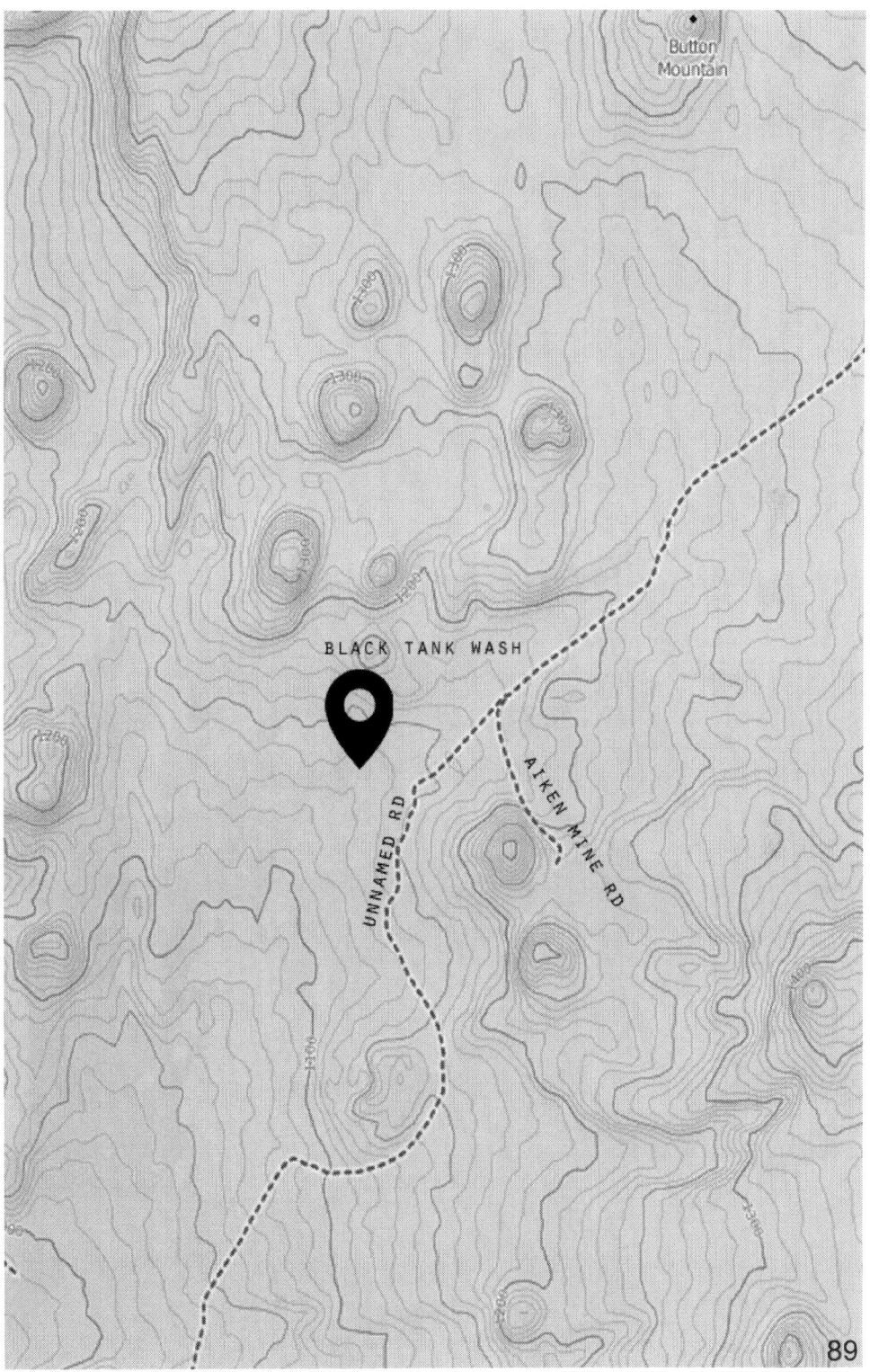

# Camp Rock Springs Petroglyphs

GPS Coordinates: 35° 9'11.78"N 115°19'42.94"W

Rock Spring is located near Round Valley, in the Mid Hills region of the Providence Mountains. Not only is the site known for its petroglyphs, but also as Camp Rock Springs, a military outpost in the 1860's.

The petroglyphs are carved in a granite boulder tank, which holds water from Rock Spring. Both the Mojave and Chemehuevi Indians are known to have used the spring, so petroglyphs are possibly from members of both tribes. The designs are mostly abstract, circles and zig-zag lines are present. A majority of the designs have a lot of wear from the elements, making them difficult to spot. A larger majority of the petroglyphs are located on the upper boulders of the tank, however a few designs can be found along the NPS created Rock Spring Loop Trail.

# Counsel Rocks Archaeological site

## GPS Coordinates: 35° 1'52.25"N 115°25'22.05"W

Counsel Rocks, is located at the base of Wild Horse Mesa, in the Mojave National Preserve. It is comprised of seven large volcanic boulders, each containing petroglyphs and/or pictographs. This site is believed to have been an ancient ceremonial site to the Chemehuevi and Mohave people who once lived upon these lands.

"Womb Rock," likely played a significant role in the Native people's ceremonies. The large hollowed out boulder contains two natural rock windows, the window facing east/west, you are able to observe the spring equinox; the sun directly penetrates through the window. In Chemehuevi mythology, there is the story of the Lone Woman in the Cave, on the spring equinox, she is penetrated by the sun. When this happens, it was believed that it would bring a fertile spring.

The interior of "Womb Rock" has numerous petroglyph designs, the most significant are those that continue to tell the fertility tale of the Lone Woman of the Cave. Directly below the window rock, where the rays of the sun would penetrate during the spring equinox are designs that are believed to represent a penis, vagina, and a flower (see above image).

The other boulders at Counsel Rocks have many additional pictograph and petroglyph panels. Some have very small designs, and others an extensive collection.

The boulder pictured above is hollow on this inside, once you crawl through the naturally carved doorway, there is a room full of pictographs; painted in red, black and white. Many are clearly visible, while others have faded to the point that you have to utilize a special software when processing your images to be able to see the full-scale of what is hidden, from the years of weathering.

It isn't clear how long ago this site was in use, nor for how long it was used by the Native people. What is clear is that it played an important part in a ritual that was very important to these people; so much so that there are additional sites scattered throughout their territory dedicated to this same belief/myth.

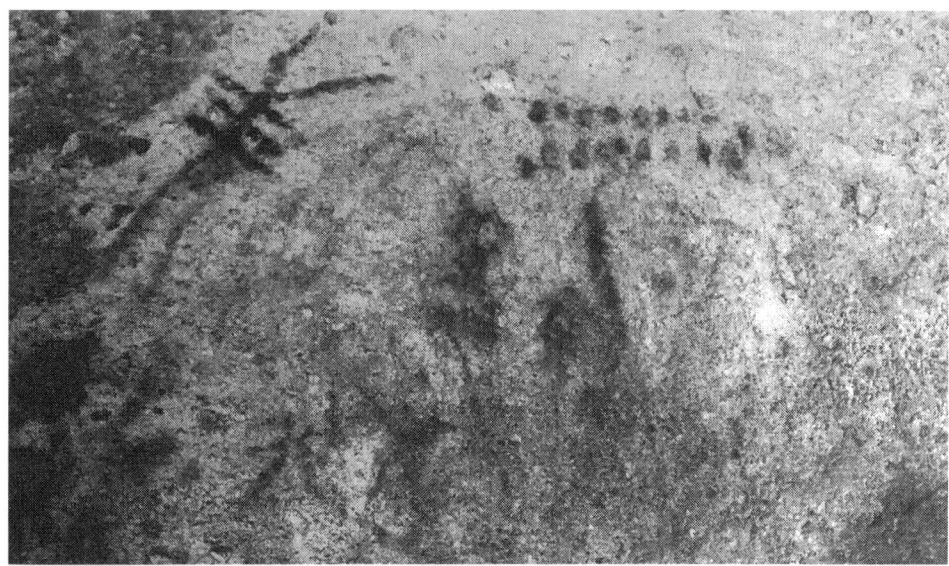

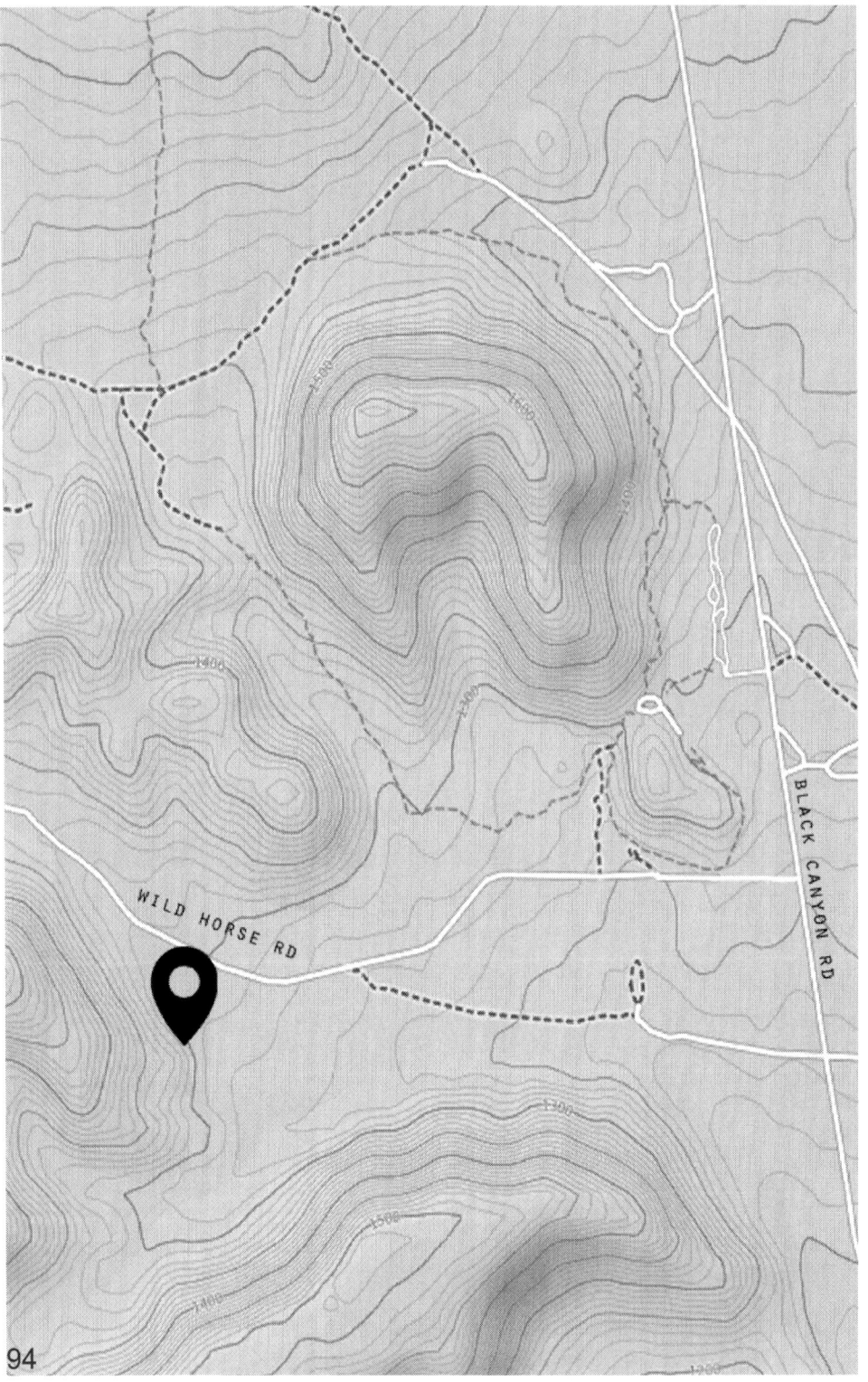

# Fort Piute / Beale

## GPS Coordinates: 35° 6'53.68"N 114°59'6.14"W

Fort Piute was established in 1859, by Captain James H. Carleton, of the 1st Dragoons. The fort was originally given the name Fort Beale, after Lieutenant Edward F. Beale of the U.S. Navy. Beale had explored this region of the desert from 1857-1859, with a caravan of camels, in an effort to establish the route for a wagon road, and to open up this portion of the west for miners and settlers, making their way west.

Fort Beale, as well as a number of additional military posts and camps had been established by Carleton, these outposts are strung along the Mojave Road, which at the time was the only established route through this portion of the Mojave Desert. The outposts had been created to give settlers safe passage from the hostile native people who had lived on these lands for hundreds of years prior.

The fort was built from local rock, at least three buildings had been built as part of Fort Beale, the largest (60 feet by 25 feet) of which consisted of three rooms, which included a storehouse, corral and quarters. Rifle ports had been built into the walls, and deflecting shields in front of the buildings doors to prevent direct fire through the opening.

This fort along with many other posts along the new travel route were abandoned by the military at the start of the Civil War. A group of volunteer soldiers, the California Volunteers, manned the outposts as often as possible after the U.S. military had pulled out. For travelers along this route, this made it a dangerous place to be. The Piute Creek Indians, still considered this their land, and regularly attacked or stole livestock from those passing through.

In 1866, after the completion of the Civil War, due to protest by local settlers, and the fact that the Mojave Road had become a U.S. Mail route, Fort Beale was reopened, and renamed Fort Piute. The fort remained occupied until 1868, when it was abandoned for good.

Today, the stone walls of two buildings remain. The walls of these buildings have been reconstructed by the HistoriCorps, a group that is dedicated to the preservation of historic places. They used the original stones from the building, and earthen mortars, from the site to hold the stone walls together. Well worn hiking trails lead through the historic fort, and the surrounding area.

# Indian Well Petroglyphs

GPS Coordinates: 35° 8'43.60"N 115° 9'32.20"W

Indian Well is located in central Lanfair Valley. The Mojave Road is located just south of this site, previous to this route being used by white people making their way across the Mojave Desert, the route was used as a prehistoric trade route for the native people along the Colorado River and those along the Pacific coast. Indian Well with its natural well would have been one of few places for travelers of this route to obtain water.

The largest concentration of petroglyphs are on the basalt outcropping directly above and beside the well. There are however scattered petroglyphs within 100 feet of the well in both directions. In all there are likely 500 – 600 petroglyphs at this site, the largest majority of which are abstract designs, in the form of circles, lines, and gridded lines. There are both anthropomorph and zoomorph designs as well, but far fewer than the abstract.

Despite being located in Chemehuevi territory, the designs are a mixture of Chemehuevi and Mohave designs. The thicker and more symmetrical designs are character features found mostly in designs created by the Mohave Indians. Other designs may be present from even earlier groups of people that inhabited these lands before the Chemehuevi.

The site is well-preserved, with minimal vandalism. There are a few inscriptions from early white travels with dates ranging from 1900-1919. The natural well still holds water, however stagnant and green in color.

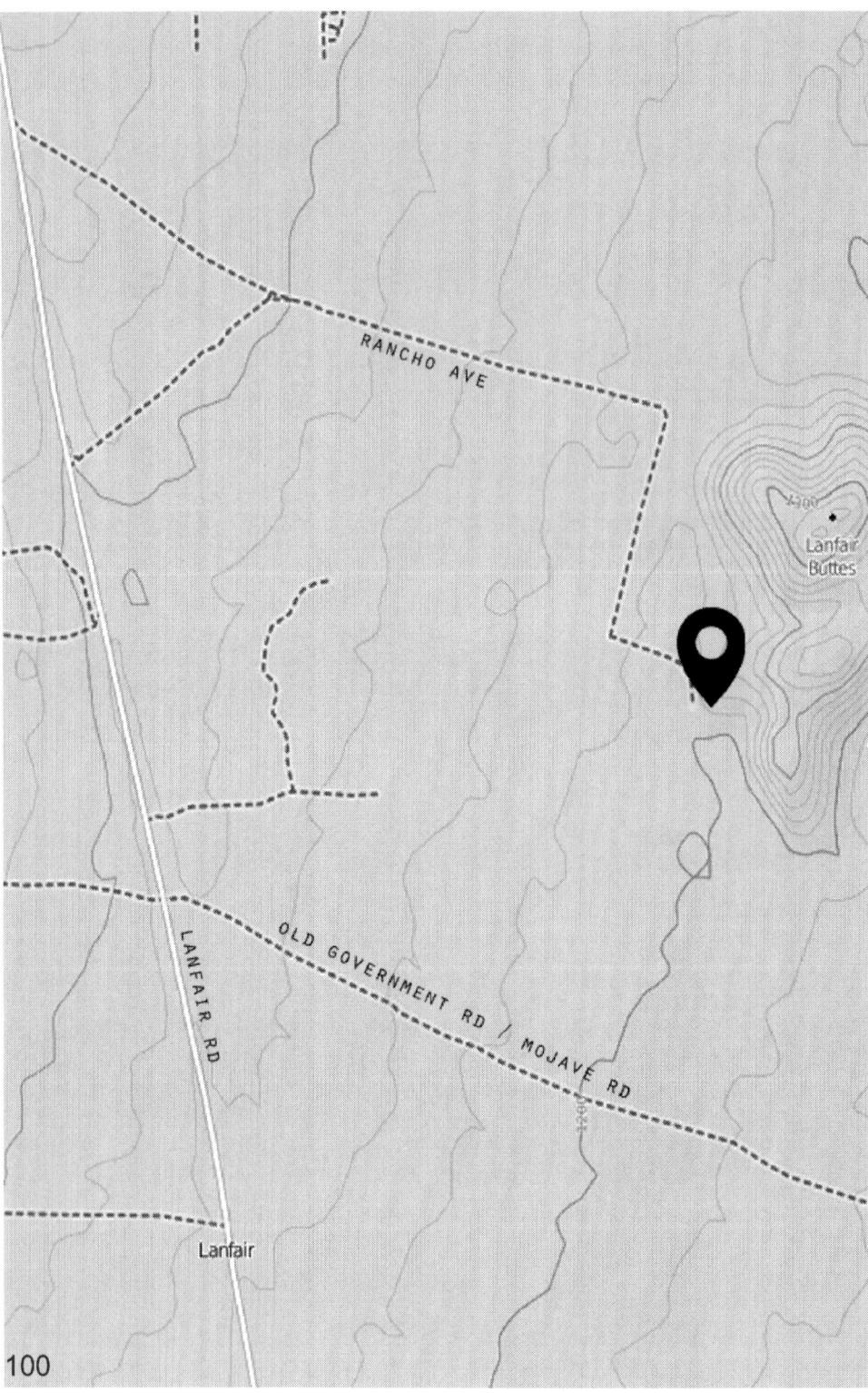

# Maruba / Ledge (Ox Cattle Company)

## GPS Coordinates: 35°12'9.72"N 115°12'9.27"W

The town of Ledge, CA was settled in the early 1900's as a farming community and railroad station on the Atchison, Topeka and Santa Fe Railroad in Lanfair Valley. The town only ever consisted of a dozen or so buildings. When the town applied for a post office, they were denied, due to another California community that had already been granted a post office under the name of Ledge. The town reapplied using the name Maruba, CA, which was accepted.

The town eventually folded, and the land that Ledge once stood on became a cattle farm, which would eventually be known as the OX Cattle Company. The OX operated for many years, under a few different ownerships, it eventually succumbed to mounting environmental pressure in the 1990's. The land was sold to the Mojave National Preserve in 2000. The cattle company buildings, water tanks, and fences remain today.

This little outpost in the middle of the Eastern Mojave Desert is used today by the Preserve for its Artist in Residence program. Depending on who the current artist in residence is, you may be able to get a personal tour of the grounds, and buildings.

Only one building remains from the Ledge era, it has been stabilized and left in a state of arrested decay.

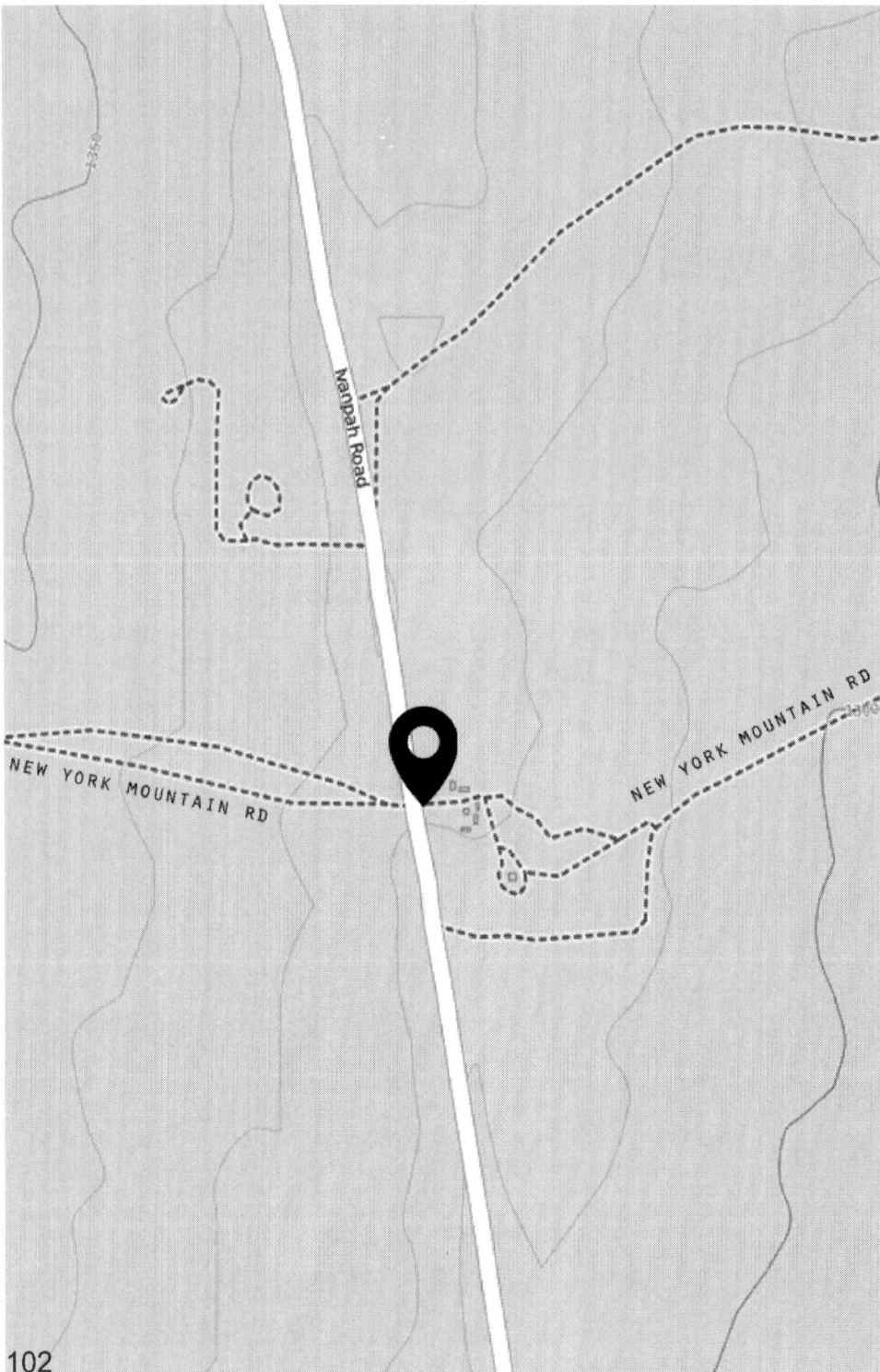

# Mary's Cave Pictographs

## GPS Coordinates: 35° 1'46.28"N 115°25'26.76"W

Located along the base of Wild Horse Mesa, and well off the beaten path for most visitors, Mary's Cave has managed to stay well-preserved and vandalism free with the exception of an inscription dated 1934.

The cave shelter measures well over three yards. Both the inside wall and ceiling contain pictographs in red pigment. A large quantity of the designs are faint, but visible without any sort of enhancements. Beside the shelter is a natural depression that was caused by many years of water running off of the mesa. The depression would collect water, making it ever more inhabitable to the Natives. In later years this depression in the stone was dammed-up by a rancher to provide water for their nearby ranch.

The cave falls within Chemehuevi territory, but it is possible that the Mohave inhabited the shelter as well. Both tribes tended to utilize the same area despite their traditional territories.

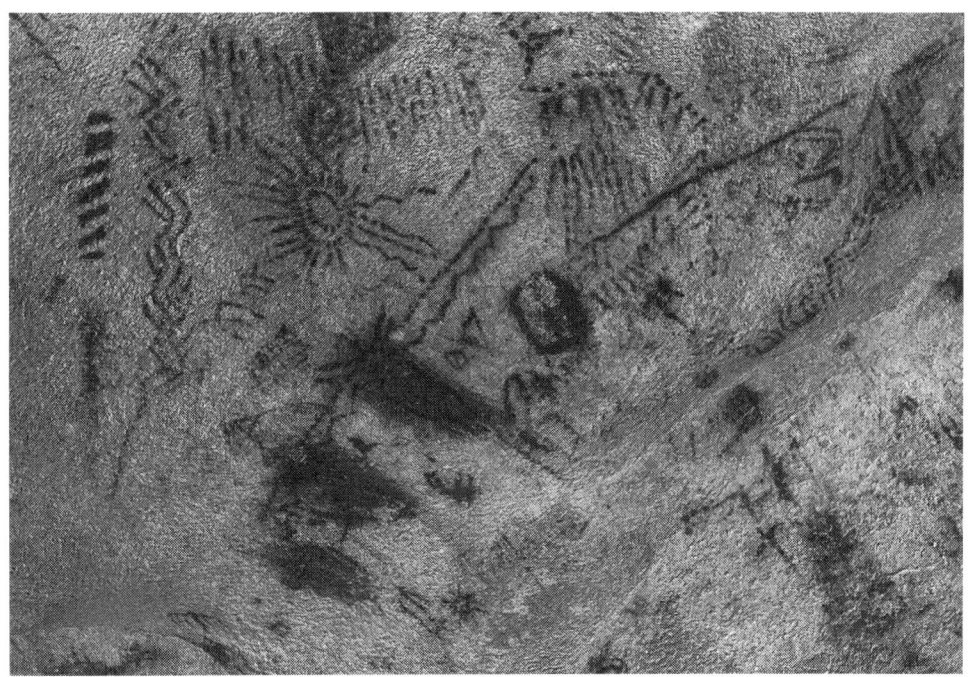

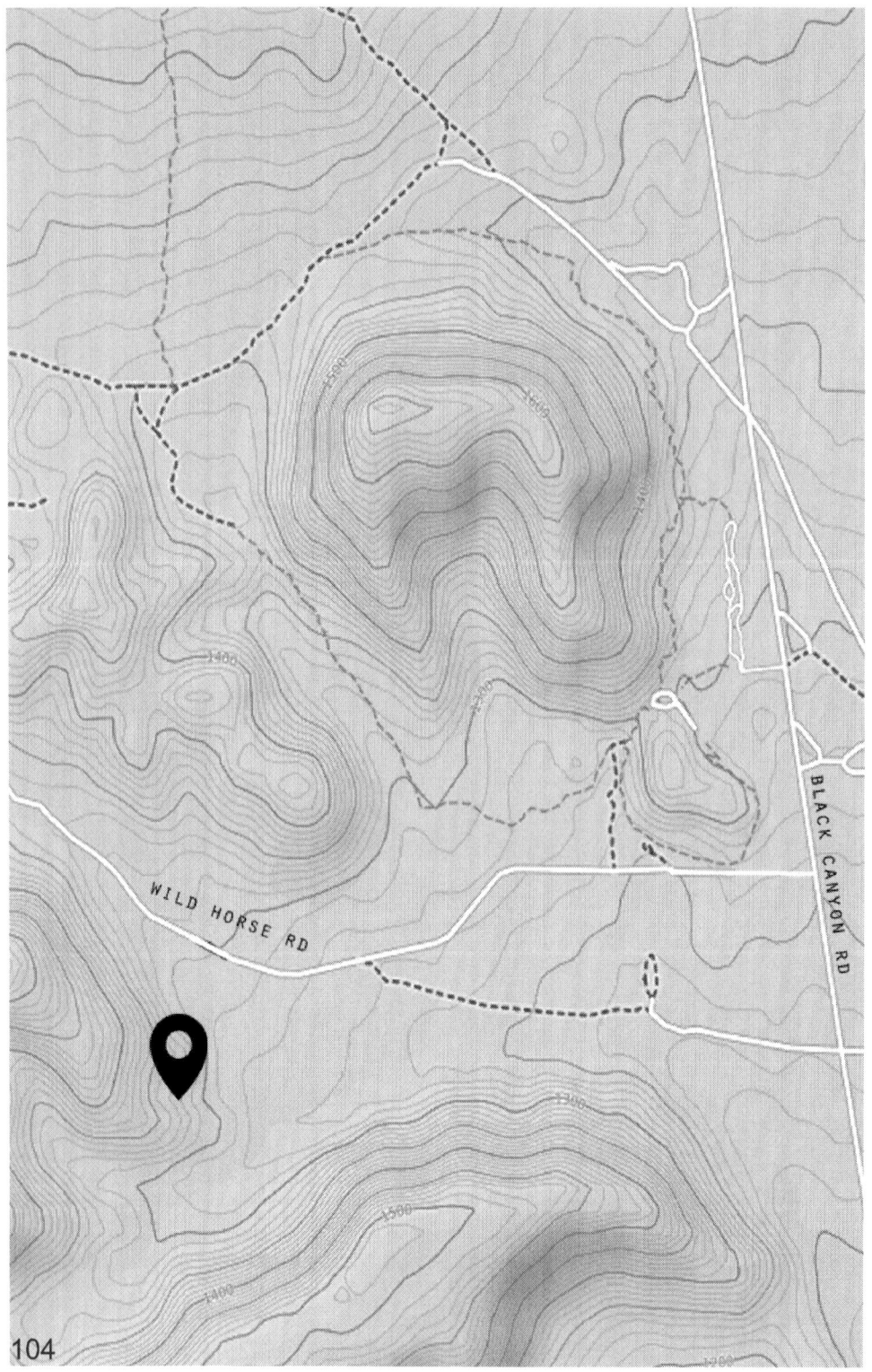

# Piute Creek Petroglyphs

## GPS Coordinates: 35° 6'50.30"N 114°58'41.12"W

Long before the Mojave Road was used by white settlers to cross the Mojave Desert, this route was used by the native people to travel between the Mojave Desert and the Colorado River. Evidence of this trail, in the form of petroglyphs (ie: rock art) can be found at the many springs and natural wells that are found along the route. Piute Creek, which was taken from the native people in the late 1850's by the U.S. military, in order to establish Fort Beale (later renamed Fort Piute), was one of these watering holes.

Water still flows at Piute Creek, it is the only stream that flows year-round in the Mojave National Preserve. Cottonwood trees dot the bank of the stream, while yucca, cholla cactus, and other desert plants thrive in surrounding Piute Canyon.

Archeological evidence has shown that the area around Piute Creek had been in use by humans for as long as several thousand years. The Native people may have very likely planted crops of corn, melons, and other edibles along the banks of this creek.

Piute Creek feel within the territory of the Chemehuevi, the southern-most branch of the Piute. Their traditional territory spanned the High Desert from the Colorado River on the east to the Tehachapi Mountains on the west and from the Las Vegas area -

and Death Valley on the north to the San Bernardino and San Gabriel Mountains in the south. Despite being the territory of the Chemehuevi, it is more than likely that the petroglyphs found along Piute Creek was placed here by various tribes, because of the established trade route. This would likely include the Mohave (whom lived in Chemehuevi territory), and even the Anasazi (Four-Corners region), as evidence has placed them in the area from 500 – 1000 A.D., trading for turquoise.

Whomever was here, left behind many messages from the past, sadly for those of us today, these messages can not be properly translated; but they can still be enjoyed in the form of an art and/or ancient language.

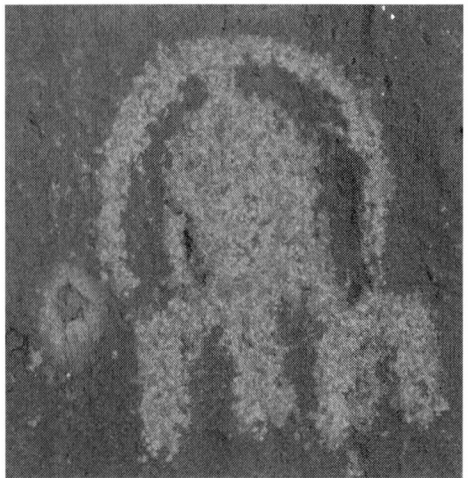
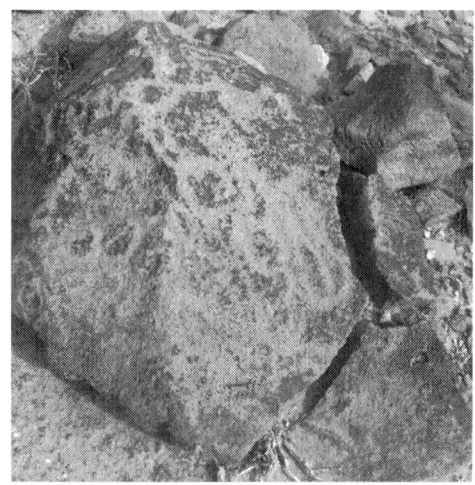

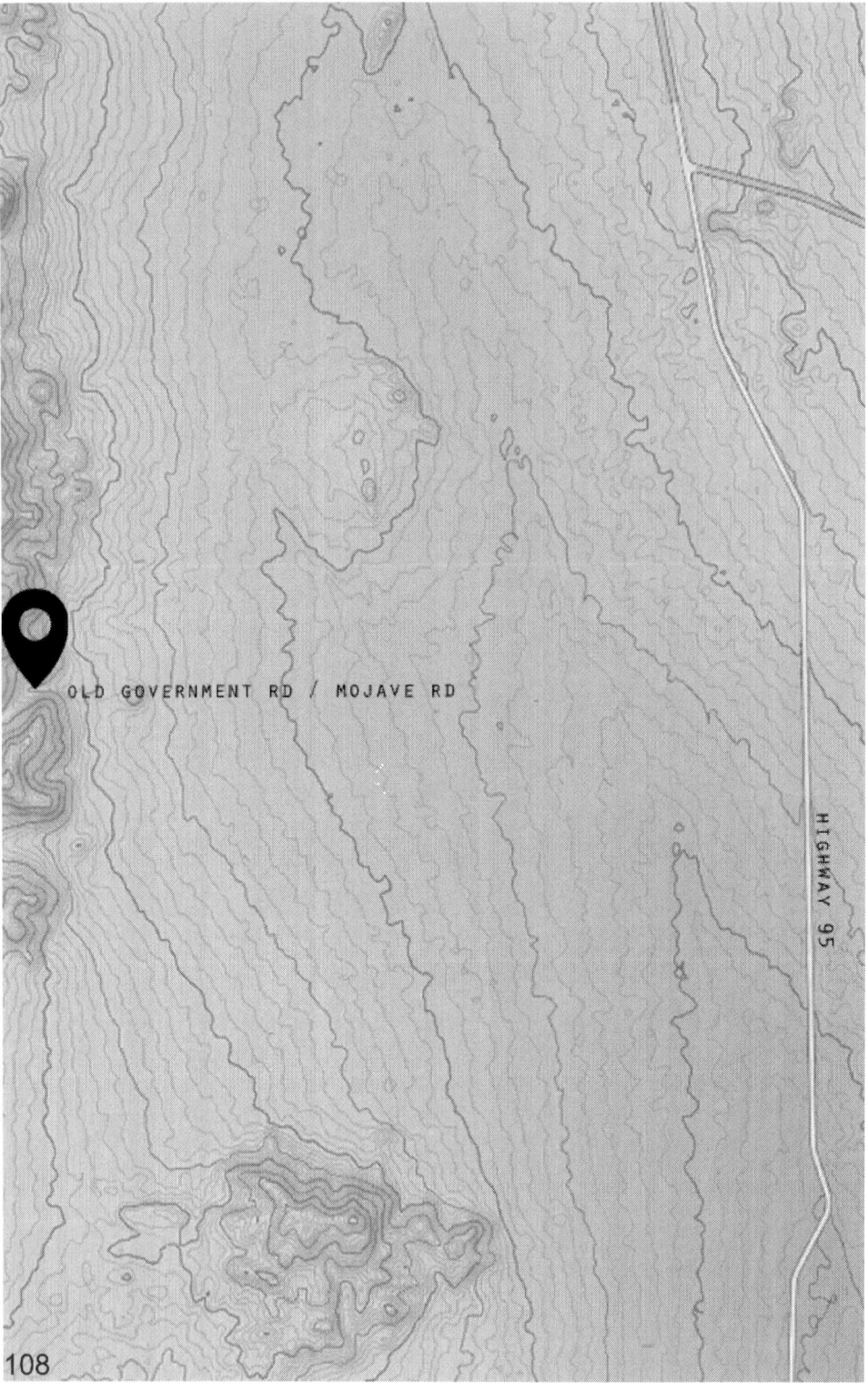

# Providence / Bonanza King Mine

## GPS Coordinates: 34°58'55.13"N 115°30'20.74"W

The ghost of Providence is situated on the rugged eastern slope of the Providence Mountain Range in the Mojave National Preserve. The town grew around the extremely successful silver mine, the Bonanza King Mine. In the spring 1880, George Goreman and P. Dwyer discovered silver at this site while out prospecting away from their then home base of Ivanpah. The rock that they discovery assayed from $640 to $5,000 a ton.

January 1882, a rich vein of silver was discovered, it was assayed at $100 to $1,200 per ton. In order to work the vein and make it profitable a large mill would need to be constructed on site. The owners opted to sell the mine as opposed to making the investment themselves. The Bonanza King was sold to the Bonanza King Consolidated Mining Company for a reported sum of $200,000.

The Bonanza King Consolidated Mining Company, eager to begin recouping their investment, had a new hoisting works and 10-stamp mill shipped in from San Francisco. The mines now had 100-150 men working around the clock. A stockpile of 2,000 tons of ore, with a value of $230 per ton was awaiting the construction of the mill.

By 1883 Providence had become a town. A post office had opened the year prior, as well two general store, two hotels, and a saloon had begun operating. The town also boasted a few company offices, a blacksmith, wagon maker, survey office, and a contractor.

In July of 1884, the superintendent of the Bonanza King boasted, "the Bonanza King is better opened up, better worked, and we have obtained better results from the ore than any other mine in this great mineral desert. Nearly one million dollars has been taken out from the mine in 18 months and ten days."

Within a year of the release of the above statement, the Bonanza King closed down for a brief one week period, at which time the miners left. The closure was said to have been due to the falling prices of silver, but other sources point to the mistreatment and over working of the mines employees. The Calico Print (newspaper) published a letter around this same time from one of the mine workers that accused foreman H. C. Callahan and shift boss John O'Donnell of being "heartless task masters.... forcing men to work more than their health and strength will permit."

Upon reopening, the Bonanza King went from employing over 100 men, down to 15 men. They slashed the pay from $4 to $3 per day.

In June of 1885, the mill was fired up again for the first time since the closure. The company was milling 24 tons of ore a day, and in one month, 24 bars of bullion had been made. One month after beginning operation the mill burnt to the ground. The mine closed down after the fire, and the owners collected their insurance claim and walked away.

In 28 months of operation the mine had produced $1,700,000 ($42,777,773 in current value).

Despite the closing of the Bonanza King in July of 1885, the Post Office continued operating at Providence until 1892, likely to continue servicing other surrounding mines in the area.

The Bonanza King would see two additional revivals, from 1906-1907 and 1915-1920. Neither revival would see the success of the early days.

A significant portion of the town site is still visible today. The stone walls of at least a dozen buildings still stand, mostly crumbled down to three or four feet; their wooden roofs long gone. The most significant building ruin is the remains of the stone block assay office. The block walls still surrounding the concrete floor beneath. Another interesting stone structure with a metal roof, wood burning stove, a table and chairs remains as well.

The mill that is present today was erected in 1906 during one of the short-lived revivals, by the Trojan Mining Company. It isn't in the greatest condition after over 100 years of neglect, but you can still get a rough idea of what it may have looked like while it was in operation.

The Providence and Bonanza King Mine site is well worth a visit to anyone interested in mining history or ghost towns. The ruins are significant compared to most desert sites. If you visit in the summer be prepared for scorching desert, during my visit in June I recorded a temperature of 113 degrees. The road to the mine itself is recommended for those with a high clearance vehicle, 4×4 is likely not required, but the road is bumpy with large stones strung about.

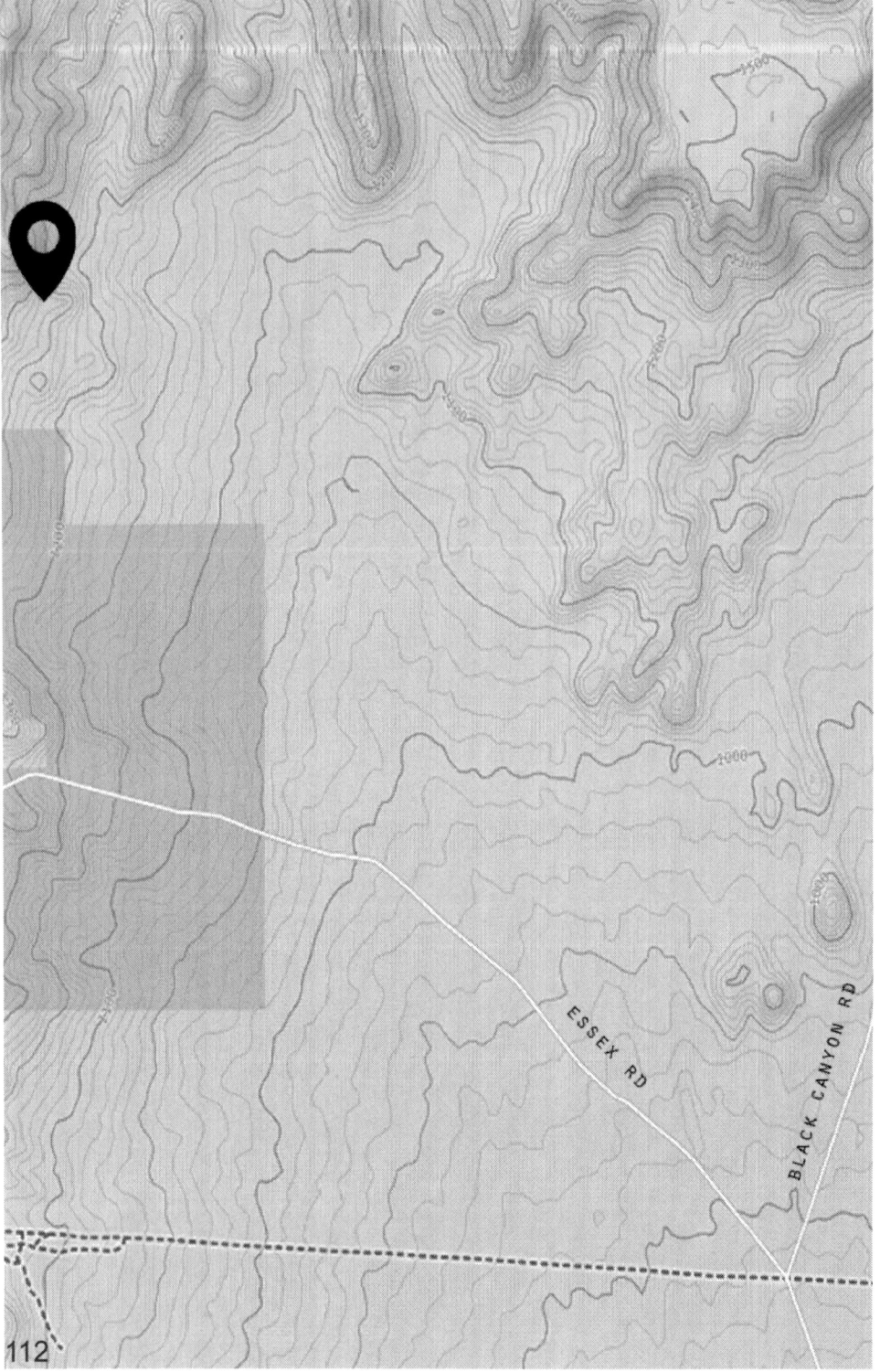

# Woods Wash Rock Art Site

GPS Coordinates:     35° 4'10.12"N 115°19'45.19"W

Woods Wash in the Woods Mountain area is a pretty remote location, even for the Preserve where everything feels remote. If you decide to wonder out and try to find this location be prepared for many miles of sketchy dirt roads, and possible dead ends. Once you reach the wilderness boundary at Woods Wash you will have to hike the rest of the way in, you will begin finding petroglyphs roughly three-quarters of a mile in. The petroglyphs are spread out over a couple of miles at the numerous basalt outcroppings that line the wash; the petroglyphs number in the thousands. There are a few faint pictographs (painted designs) at locations as well.

Like a majority of the rock art sites in the Mojave Preserve, the Woods Wash petroglyphs are a mixture of designs from both Chemehuevi and Mohave tribes, as well the possibility of an earlier man from the Archaic era (8000 to 2000 BC). The bolder lined designs are an attribute of the Mohave designs, while the narrower lined designs are accustomed to the Chemehuevi.

With the extensive number of designs, the range in style of design is extensive. While a majority are abstract designs (geometric shapes), there is everything from anthropomorph (stylized human figures), zoomorphs (animal designs).

The wash has a number of natural caves that formed out of the volcanic flow, as well as mud caves. These caves are likely the shelters used by the Natives that created this wonderland of unexplainable rock art.

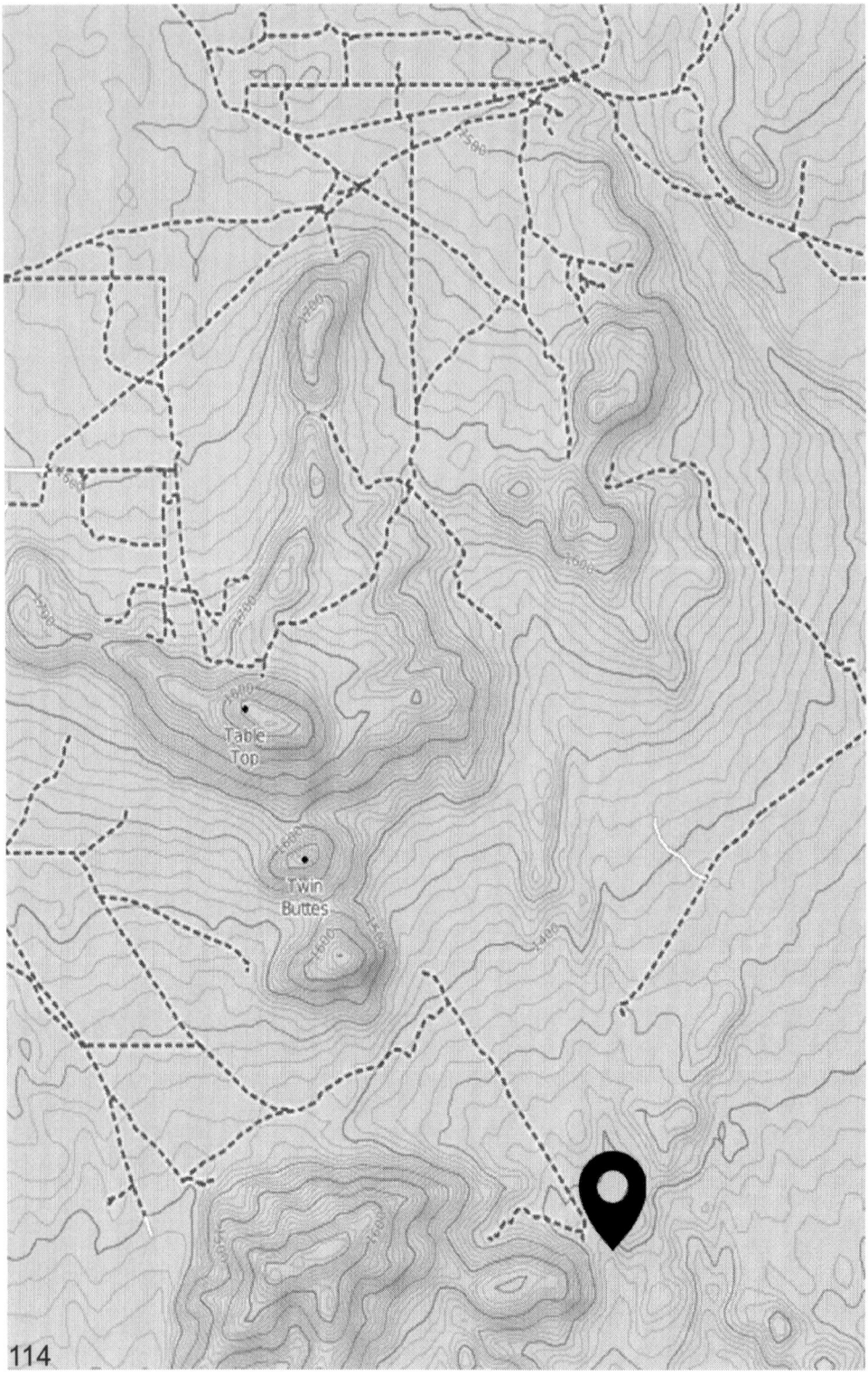

# NOTES:

Follow the authors website for trips reports, photographs and historical studies.

www.deathvalleyjim.com

# Also available by Death Valley Jim

*The Secret Places in the Mojave Desert Series*

Printed in Great Britain
by Amazon.co.uk, Ltd.,
Marston Gate.